CRUDE OIL PIPE LINES AND COMPETITION IN THE OIL INDUSTRY

This is the second in a series of studies on competition and monopoly in American industry financed by a grant from the Merrill Foundation for the Advancement of Financial Knowledge. The series has been planned to include a number of studies focusing on the effectiveness of competition in particular industrial markets accompanied by certain investigations into the effect on competition of various elements of market structure and business practice common to many industries. Although each volume is an independent study representing only the views of its author, all are expected to contribute to the central objective of the whole project: an evaluation of monopoly policy in the United States.

CRUDE OIL PIPE LINES

AND COMPETITION IN THE OIL INDUSTRY

LESLIE COOKENBOO, JR.
Assistant Professor of Economics
The Rice Institute

Harvard University Press
Cambridge, Massachusetts
1955

O.P.

Distributed in Great Britain by

GEOFFREY CUMBERLEGE
OXFORD UNIVERSITY PRESS
LONDON

Library of Congress Catalog Card Number 55-10968
Printed in the United States of America

PREFACE

Much of the research for this study was originally carried out in 1952. Extensive revisions with some additional research were made in the summer and fall of 1953, and minor changes were made in the fall of 1954. During this period numerous organizations and individuals have contributed to the preparation of the study. A list in more or less chronological order follows:

The capital costs used in computing the cost curves in Chapter I were determined as part of the Petroleum Research Project of the Rice Institute Department of Economics and Business Administration for the United States Air Force and the Bureau of Mines. I am indebted to the project staff, particularly to Allen F. Rhodes, who was (1) the co-designer of the computation process for the capital costs and (2) my tutor in the mysteries of pipe-line hydraulics.

This study is an abridgment and revision of a doctoral thesis in the Department of Economics and Social Science at the Massachusetts Institute of Technology.[1] The research director was Professor Morris A. Adelman, who contributed much more than was required in the line of duty in the matter of reading and criticizing the manuscripts of both the original and the revised versions.

The revision of the thesis was made possible by a grant from the School of Industrial Management at the Massachusetts Institute of Technology. It is difficult to overestimate the importance of such grants by the Sloan School. They enable academic personnel to engage in the financial luxury of a summer devoted entirely to the revision and organization of manuscript — something

[1] L. Cookenboo, Jr., Economies of Scale in the Operation of Crude Oil Pipe Lines, unpublished doctoral thesis deposited in the Library of the Massachusetts Institute of Technology (1953).

that can be done much more efficiently on a full-time basis than on part-time.

My thanks go to the following persons who have read and criticized all or part of the original or revised manuscripts: Dean Edward S. Mason; Dr. Richard J. Gonzalez; Dr. Fredrick T. Moore and other members of the Inter-Industry Analysis Branch of the Office of Chief Economist of the Bureau of Mines; Professors J. E. Hodges, Carl Kaysen, J. B. Giles, J. H. Auten, and K. R. Wadleigh; and the staff members of the Rice Petroleum Research Project.

At various times typing assistance was provided by the Department of Economics and Business Administration of the Rice Institute and by the School of Business Administration of the University of California.

Finally, and perhaps most important from the point of view of the book proper, publication was made possible by a grant from Dean Mason's Merrill Foundation grant for public policy studies.

It is probably unnecessary to add that none of the gentlemen and organizations listed above should be held responsible for any errors or opinions with which the reader may not agree.

Leslie Cookenboo, Jr.

Berkeley, California
December 1, 1954

CONTENTS

TABLES

CHARTS

FIGURES

CRUDE OIL PIPE LINES AND COMPETITION IN THE OIL INDUSTRY

INTRODUCTION

Since the late years of the last century, there has been a continual expression of dissatisfaction with the alleged dominance and control of the oil industry by the major oil companies. This criticism was at first directed at the single large company, "that international outlaw the Standard Oil Company." [1] During the Senate debates on the Sherman Act in 1890, Standard was singled out for attack as one of the chief offenders among the trusts. Senator Reagan cited a case where the Standard Oil Company endeavored to "crush" an independent refiner. Standard forced the railroad which carried both the competitor's and Standard's crude (in this area) to transport Standard's oil for ten cents per barrel while charging the competitor thirty-five cents; the extra twenty-five cents was then paid to Standard.[2]

This dominance of the industry was said to rest principally upon the large company's ownership of most of the pipe-line facilities, especially of the crude oil trunk lines. The mechanism by which Standard forced the rebate just mentioned was a threat to build a pipe line for its own oil parallel to the railroad.[3] Through its pipe-line ownership the Standard Oil Company in its time was said to "hold the entire oil industry of the country by the throat." [4] This strangle hold via pipe lines caused serious problems for the small companies. For example, independent producers located in fields far from refining centers had no access to independent refineries at those centers except through Standard's pipe lines. They had the alternative, so it is said, of either refining crude for limited local markets or selling it to Standard

[1] 40 *Congressional Record* 2163 (February 6, 1906). Remarks of Representative Stanley of Kentucky. This company, the old Standard Oil Company of New Jersey, is not to be confused with the existing companies called "Standard."

[2] 21 *Congressional Record* 2457 (March 21, 1890).

[3] 21 *Congressional Record* 2457 (March 21, 1890).

[4] 40 *Congressional Record* 7000 (May 17, 1906). Remarks of Senator Lodge.

(or its pipe lines) at Standard's price: "Those well owners are absolutely at the mercy of the pipe lines . . . A small well owner is compelled to take the price that is offered by the controller of the trunk line." [5]

At the other end of the crude trunk line, independent refineries at market centers had no direct access to the independent producers at the distant points of production. Any oil carried for these refineries was carried by Standard. If an independent refiner located at a market bought oil in the field, he could either ship his oil in the Standard pipe line (if permitted) or use much more costly overland transportation. The large company allegedly charged exorbitant rates on any oil carried for others and used the great pipe-line profits resulting to subsidize its own refineries, which could then undersell the independents. "Standard Oil profits immensely by . . . rates which are so arranged as to give it an overwhelming advantage over its independent competitors." [6]

Under such conditions the independent refiner helped drive himself out of business every time he used Standard's transportation facilities. If the independent refiner chose not to buy in the field, but to buy instead from Standard at the refinery site, he paid Standard's price for crude. This price was allegedly kept high; consequently the profits from crude sales could also be used to help drive the independent refiners and the dealers they supplied out of business.

> The Standard Oil Company purchases oil from the independent shipping oil . . . and holds a monopoly of the use of the main line; and unless it is put under the control of the Interstate Commerce Commission, it can carry on its business with impunity and practically destroy all independent dealers . . .[7]

One other alternative was available to the producer or refiner who had no transportation facilities and wished to escape the

[5] 40 *Congressional Record* 6366 (May 4, 1906). Remarks of Senator Lodge.

[6] 40 *Congressional Record* 6358 (May 4, 1906). Message to the Senate from Theodore Roosevelt.

[7] 40 *Congressional Record* 7001 (May 17, 1906). Remarks of Senator Nelson.

grasp of the "international outlaw." This was defensive vertical integration, in this case the building of the firm's own pipe lines. Defensive vertical integration began early in the history of the industry and still continues. However, it was a rather expensive undertaking for many of the small companies; as a result, relatively few were able to escape Standard's domination by this method. One of the most notable instances of defensive integration, one in which there was a certain amount of poetic justice, occurred after the dissolution of Standard. The larger independents then existing (Gulf, Pure, Texas Company, and others) were so well integrated (as defensive measures against Standard) that the newly separated Standard companies found themselves at somewhat of a competitive disadvantage and therefore found it necessary to engage in defensive vertical integration themselves.

Legislative reaction in Congress against Standard's pipe-line ownership appeared as early as 1906. In commenting on his Hepburn Act amendment which made pipe lines common carriers, Senator Lodge states specifically that its purpose was to curb the power of the Standard Oil Company: "My object, I state frankly, in this amendment is to bring the pipe lines of the Standard Oil Company within the jurisdiction of the Interstate Commerce Commission." [8]

The criticism of concentrated ownership of pipe lines did not stop with the antitrust dissolution of the old Standard Oil Company in 1911.[9] It was merely transferred to the several large companies which developed after that time. Complaints were widespread in the depression years of the 1930's and have recently appeared again. Professor Wolbert has found that bills to divorce pipe lines were introduced in every session of Congress from the 71st (1931) through the 79th (1945).[10] During the TNEC hearings (1939–40), one witness described graphically the plight of the independent refiner in the industry:

[8] 40 *Congressional Record* 7000 (May 17, 1906).

[9] See *Standard Oil of New Jersey* v. *U.S.*, 221 U.S. 1 (1911).

[10] See G. S. Wolbert, Jr., *American Pipe Lines* (Norman, Okla., 1952), p. 4, fn. 4. The controversy was renewed in E. V. Rostow, *A National Policy for the Oil Industry* (New Haven, 1948).

My father went into the oil business in 1888. He was a small refiner nearly all of the active years of his business life. He acquired a plant (Chicago) in 1904. It was an old varnish plant, and he made it over into an oil refinery. Now, I can only tell you gentlemen what my father told me . . . Repeatedly he tried to get the Standard Oil Company, whose pipe line was about 600 yards from his refinery, to transport oil from Oklahoma to that refinery in Chicago.

Now the Standard Oil Company, the pipe line company, didn't arbitrarily say, "We won't transport your oil."

They gave him a much more conclusive answer for [*sic*] that. They said, "We just haven't got room in the line." And so for many years he transported every barrel of his crude oil from Oklahoma to Chicago and refined that oil, paying therefor the going rate of freight over the rails . . . How did he keep going with such a disadvantage? He nearly starved to death for a good many years, until in 1914 he went down to Oklahoma in flush production and made one of those luck crude oil contracts for 3 or 4 years, and it pulled him out of the woods, and that is all that saved him. And it was a good enough contract to overcome all the transportation difficulties, and when that contract was over he pulled up stakes and quit, and hasn't been in the business since, or he would have lost it all.[11]

This supposedly was the almost inevitable state of the independent refiner located at the market who tried to compete with refineries which had cheap pipe-line transportation for their crude oil.

The same testimony also provides an apt description of the plight of the independent producer, especially in times of bonanza fields and flush production before the introduction of production control in the mid-1930's. In 1914 and 1915 there was a period of flush production in the Mid-Continent fields. The resulting problems faced by the independent producers were typical.

At the outset of the industry in the southwest . . . the development of producing fields was very rapid and the shift of . . . supplies was transcontinental from the East to the Southwest. The pipe lines were built to carry oil from the Southwestern fields to the market refineries by the majors.

. . . . .

[11] Testimony of J. E. Shatford (an independent refiner, once petroleum coordinator of the NRA), TNEC *Hearings,* Part 15, pp. 8158 ff.

Now here were a lot of producers in the Southwest with oil on their hands, wells flowing, nowhere to put the oil, and here there was at the market a rapidly advancing demand for petroleum products that the major companies couldn't meet because they didn't have the refining capacity. The result was that there was a wide-open field for the entry of additional refiners.

Well, the refiner[12] [*sic*] who had surplus crude had one of two choices: he could put it in the pipe line or he could run it down the creek. The third alternative was to build a refinery and make his own permanent market, and when he reached that decision he had to make it on the basis of practical circumstances, not on the basis of law. He couldn't very well put his oil into a pipe that wouldn't take it, and so he built his refinery at the only place he could. He needed to act.

Now it was under these circumstances — and I don't mean to imply that that affected every refinery alike. Some refiners would have built in the field under any circumstances, some would not have built in the field, it is only reasonable to assume that most of them would have followed the much wiser leadership of the major companies and have built at the market.

But they built where they needed to build, and at that point, and at that time the organic structure of the refining industry was developed.[13]

Such has been the alleged plight of the independent (that is, non-integrated) company in the oil industry for fifty or sixty years. There is nothing really unique about such criticisms of the major oil companies. Alcoa, for instance, was accused of using a vertical integration squeeze based on its control of ingot production.[14] It supposedly sold sheet to fabricators at a price lower than the sum of the price of ingots and the cost of rolling. This left competing sheet producers who paid the market price for ingots at a competitive disadvantage.

There is no dearth of respectable economic reasoning to support the validity of such complaints, if not the justice of the remedies sought. Where one company (or small group) in an industry controls one vertical stage of that industry completely, it is in a position to abuse its less fortunate competitors in the

[12] "Refiner" should probably read "producer."
[13] TNEC *Hearings,* Part 15, pp. 8157–8158.
[14] See *U.S.* v. *Aluminum Company of America,* 148 Fd(2) 416 (1945).

earlier or later stages. Acting as a single or joint monopsonist it can exploit the earlier stages of the industry, and as a monopolist the later stages. Such can easily be the economic facts of life in a vertically organized industry; and such, it is said, have been and are the facts of life to the independent producers and refiners in the oil industry, especially to independent refiners. (Independent producers do not complain so much any more, since their price is now protected against catastrophic declines by the state governmental agencies' production control — a control system which has, to date, remained free from anti-trust prosecution.)

To what extent is the petroleum industry actually controlled through the ownership of crude oil pipe lines? What remedies for this control have been proposed? What remedies are feasible and desirable? May the real problem be quite different from that traditionally discussed? It is with these questions that this inquiry, which is divided into four sections, will be concerned.

A prerequisite to a discussion of public policy for any industry is a knowledge of the cost conditions under which the industry operates. It is invalid to propose any form of regulation for an industry (for example, an alternative structure) without first determining the costs peculiar to the existing and proposed firms. Are there economies or dis-economies of scale? (That is, do large plants have lower per-unit costs than small plants?) Do per-unit costs for individual plants rise or fall with output? Are there economies or dis-economies of integration? Quantitative cost analysis is time-consuming and an often painful process; but without it there is no way of evaluating the economic consequences of policies designed to reorganize or otherwise regulate industries. Advocacy of an industrial public policy without the data necessary to predict its effects on costs of production is indefensible.

Although crude oil pipe lines have been a subject of some controversy for sixty or seventy years, the attackers and defenders of major ownership of the lines have neither provided nor used adequate cost data in their commentaries. Consequently, a cost study was carried out for this investigation. It is summarized in Chapter I.

In addition to costs, it is also necessary to know the structure of an industry before discussing its regulation. ("Structure" in this sense refers to the ownership, size, and location of the industry's capacity.) It may also be necessary to determine, in part at least, the structure of the industries from which the industry under consideration buys and to which it sells. Such information is necessary in the case of crude pipe lines for both the refining and producing stages of the oil industry, as well as for the pipe lines themselves. As in the case of costs, adequate data have not been presented by past commentators. As a result, the second chapter of this inquiry is devoted to a statistical analysis of relevant company capacity and locational data.

The controversy over crude oil pipe lines as exemplified in the comments of two recent writers is summarized and evaluated in Chapter III; in the course of this evaluation recent earnings and price (that is, rate) policies of the pipe lines are discussed. In the final chapter the necessary goals of any public policy toward crude oil pipe lines are set out. In addition, this chapter includes an appraisal of industry performance in the light of these goals and a proposal for public policy.

I

COSTS OF OPERATION OF CRUDE OIL TRUNK LINES

This chapter will be concerned with a discussion of long-, short-, and intermediate-run costs of operating crude oil pipe lines. For the benefit of the reader not conversant with economic jargon, it might be well to begin with a description of the three cost categories. It is essential that they be understood, since much of the argument in Chapter IV is based on the cost curves to be described here.

First, it is necessary to distinguish between the various types of costs that may be considered under any of these three categories. "Total" cost (be it long-, short-, or intermediate-run) is the total expenditure necessary for producing a given output. "Average" cost is the cost per unit of producing a given output; it is equal to total cost divided by output. For example, if the total expenditure for an ouput of 100 units is $1000, then total cost is $1000 and average cost (per-unit cost) is $10 per unit ($1000 divided by 100 units). "Marginal" cost is the change in total cost associated with changes in output. If 100 units cost $1000 and 101 units cost $1008, then "marginal" cost is $8 (the change in total cost divided by the change in output). "Fixed" and "variable" costs are simply parts of total (or average) cost. Fixed costs are those incurred even when no output is produced, for example, interest on the money borrowed to buy machinery, pay taxes, and so forth. Variable costs (out-of-pocket costs) are expenditures that would not be necessary were no output produced, for example, expenditures for labor and raw materials. Total cost is equal to the sum of total fixed cost and total variable cost. Average cost is equal to the sum of average fixed cost and average variable cost.

A "short-run" cost curve shows the cost of producing various outputs with a given amount of fixed capital equipment. In other words, it is the cost curve for a given size of plant, the output of which can be changed simply by using more or less labor and raw materials. Changes in short-run costs with changes in output represent changes in expenditures for items of variable cost *only;* no extra machinery or other capital equipment is needed to increase output.

Figure 1

LONG- AND SHORT-RUN AVERAGE COST CURVES

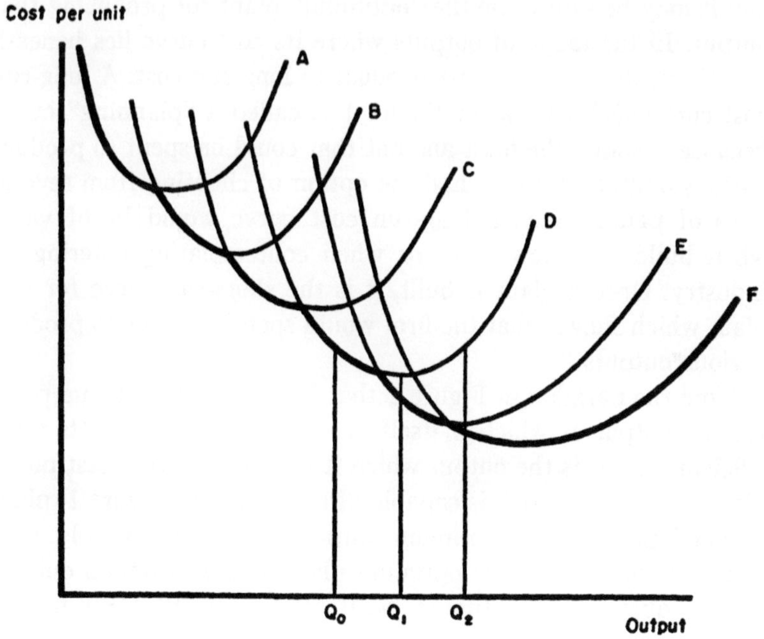

A long-run cost curve (also called a "planning" curve) is an "envelope" of all possible short-run curves. It shows the least possible expenditure for producing any output. That is, it takes into account all individual plant cost curves in order to determine which plant can produce each output for the least amount possible (relative to all other plants). This is illustrated in Figure 1.

This diagram shows per-unit cost plotted against output (the short-run cost curves) for each of six possible plants ("A"–"F") that might be used to produce some product. The long-run average cost curve is the envelope of these short-run curves (the heavy, wavy line). (If there were an infinite number of plants possible, then the long-run curve would be continuous, not wavy.) It shows the least possible expenditure for any given output in the range of outputs under consideration. Output Q_0 might be produced with either plant "A," "B," "C," "D," "E," or "F." However, D's short-run cost curve lies beneath all the others at Q_0; therefore its cost is the least possible for producing Q_0, and it may be said to be the "optimum" plant for producing that output. In the range of outputs where its cost curve lies beneath all others, its short-run cost is equal to long-run cost. A long-run cost curve such as that in Figure 1 is called a "planning" curve because it shows the least amount that could be spent to produce various outputs if a firm had the option of choosing from several sizes of plants. Such a long-run cost curve would be of value when building a new plant or when contemplating entering an industry. Once a plant is built, it is the short-run curve for this plant which shows what the firm would spend in order to produce various outputs.

Note the paradox in Figure 1 that D is *not* the optimum plant for the output at which it itself is most efficient (Q_1). Its most efficient output is the output which it produces at the least possible cost per unit that *it* is capable of achieving. In Figure 1, plant E could produce D's optimum output (Q_1) more cheaply than could D; hence E is the optimum plant at D's optimum output. It is a question of optimum *plant* relative to all *other* plants, versus optimum *output* for a *given* plant (without consideration of others) once that plant is built. Because of this paradox, any plant in Figure 1, say D, would be built originally to produce an output less than its own optimum output. Hence, it could subsequently increase its output, should it so desire, and thereby achieve a lower per-unit cost. Indeed, it could increase its output to Q_2 before average costs became higher than they were at the design output. It might be asked why a firm would ever consider producing Q_2 with D when E and F can produce it for less. If the need for Q_2 had been foreseen before any plant was built, then plant E would probably have been built. However, if the original output desired was Q_0, the correct choice would have been D. A subsequent expansion to Q_2 could then be made with plant D. This would be done instead of building a new plant if the cash costs of operating plant D at Q_2 were less than the total costs of operating plant F at Q_2.

One other "paradox" should be pointed out in Figure 1. Note that the short-run average costs decrease and then rise, even though the long-run cost curve falls throughout the range of outputs. Consequently a "U" shaped short-run average cost curve may occur for each plant while long-run average costs decline continuously.

In the range of outputs where long-run average costs decrease (in this case throughout the range), there are said to be "economies of scale." That is, by producing larger amounts conglomerately in larger plants, it is possible to achieve lower per-unit costs, better known as "mass-production economies." If the long-run average cost curve declines throughout the range of outputs, then no plant can achieve the least possible (long-run) cost of producing the product, unless there is some size of plant, say F, which is the largest possible for one reason or another. However, something approaching the least possible long-run cost can be had with the large plants, for example, E and F in Figure 1, since the average cost curve declines more and more slowly as output rises. From the point of view of both society and the firm, plants in an industry having costs such as those shown in Figure 1 should be as large as possible in order to achieve as low average costs as possible — apart from any political or sociological disadvantages of large business.

In the case of pipe lines it is also necessary to utilize the concept of "intermediate-run" costs. If the curves labeled A–F in Figure 1 were the basis of a planning curve for pipe lines, they would be called not "short-run," but "intermediate-run" pipe-line cost curves, each representing a given line size carrying various "throughputs." (Pipe-line output is called "throughput"—the volume of liquid carried per unit of time.) In some industries the output of individual plants can be expanded above the original output simply by adding more labor or raw materials; these may be described with short-run cost curves. However, in the case of pipe lines, throughput can be increased above the designed capacity only by the addition of more capital equipment (pumping stations), along with extra labor and fuel. Short-run cost curves which allow for a fixed amount of capital equipment are "reversible." That is, when output is decreased (by laying off workers and buying smaller amounts of raw materials), the short-run curve shows the appropriate cost for the lower output. On the other hand, intermediate-run cost curves which include costs of varying amounts of capital equipment are not reversible. If pipe line D (again referring to Figure 1, this time as a series of intermediate-run curves) were built for throughput Q_0, then the costs of carrying throughputs less than Q_0 in line D would *not* be shown by the curve labeled D; these costs would be higher for all throughputs less than Q_0. Why? The curve D would be based, for planning purposes, on the proper (minimum possible) number of pumping stations for each throughput. It takes more stations of a given size to push larger throughputs through a given size pipe. Consequently, the number of stations built on line D for throughput Q_0 would be larger than needed for lesser throughputs. If throughput is cut below Q_0, the number of stations cannot be cut (as could the number of workers in some other industry), since stations represent fixed capital investments—investments which incur costs even if the stations are not needed. In short, too many pumping stations would be present for any lower throughput; consequently there would be higher average costs than if the line had been designed for the lower throughput with the minimum number of stations required for that throughput. Hence, the necessity of the hybrid term "intermediate-run" in the pipe-line case. In this case the long-run curve is the envelope of the intermediate-run curves, not of the short-run curves.

With this digression into the principles of economics in mind, it is possible to proceed with the discussion of pipe-line costs. The costs computed for this study were determined primarily by the method of engineering estimation, not by the use of actual historical costs. Where engineering estimation is feasible for cost studies it should be used, since actual costs may be subject to any number of erratic variations arising from construction or operating conditions unique to particular cases. In the case of the majority of the cost items, the process of computation involved a physical determination of the amount of equipment or services required, followed by the pricing of this amount from current price quotations furnished by suppliers and/or pipe-line companies. In some cases where particular items did not readily lend themselves to a priori engineering estimation, it was necessary to use historical costs. One example of this is the construction materials cost of pumphouses, for which actual costs obtained from a pipe-line company were used as the basis of computation. This particular item also illustrates the dangers of using historical costs. The stations were built in a period of unusually bad weather; hence the labor costs were much higher than would be the case normally. The materials costs were usable, but the labor costs had to be estimated from other sources. The notable exceptions where actual costs were used as the principal basis for computation include costs of surveying the right-of-way, main-line valves, office operation, site improvement at stations, and the pipe-line communications system. Since the details of this cost study are reported elsewhere,[1] it will not be necessary to engage here in an extended discussion of such problems as optimum operating pressure, safety factor, wall thickness of pipe, centrifugal versus reciprocating pumps, diesel engines versus electric motors, and so forth. However, it is necessary to discuss in sum-

[1] See L. Cookenboo, Jr., "Costs of Operating Crude Oil Pipe Lines," *Rice Institute Pamphlet,* April 1954, pp. 35–113.

mary form certain points about pipe-line technology and the results of the cost study, since this information is all-important for the subsequent discussion.

Production function. — In order to determine costs by engineering estimation, it is necessary to compute an "engineering production function" relating the factors of production (the goods and services used to produce a product) and output. Such a function shows the possible combinations of the factors of production which can be used to produce various levels of output.

A basic choice between two "factors of production" exists in the determination of the optimum line diameter for carrying any particular throughput. A given size of line may be used for several different throughputs by applying different amounts of power (hydraulic horsepower) to the oil carried — the more horsepower, the more throughput (but less than proportionately more). Conversely, any given throughput can be achieved by the use of several possible sizes of lines with the proper amount of horsepower applied. There are, in short, variable physical proportions of these two basic factors of production, "line diameter" and "horsepower," which may be used to develop any given throughput. As a result, the management of a pipe-line company is forced to choose between several sizes of line when planning to develop a given throughput. Furthermore, the long-run cost of carrying crude oil might vary with throughput, as did the long-run costs in Figure 1. Larger throughputs might cost less or more per barrel. Managements, then, not only have the option of several sizes of line for each throughput, they also may have the option of choosing throughputs having different costs per barrel. Other things being equal, a pipe-line company planning to build a line should select the cheapest combination of line diameter and horsepower for the throughput which can be carried at the least cost per barrel.

A production function relating line diameter, horsepower, and throughput can be derived for crude oil pipe lines. Indeed, many such functions could be derived, depending on the density and viscosity of the oil carried, the wall thickness of pipe used, and so forth. However, for the purposes of this monograph one function will suffice. The only differences among the cost curves derived from different functions are in absolute dollars per barrel-mile for each throughput, not in the relative positions of the intermediate-run cost curves for each line. The latter is the important point for public policy considerations. A crude oil trunk pipe-line production function is shown in Chart 1. This

Chart 1

PRODUCTION FUNCTION FOR CRUDE OIL TRUNK PIPE LINES: LINE DIAMETER VERSUS HORSEPOWER VERSUS THROUGHPUT – 1000 MILE LINES*

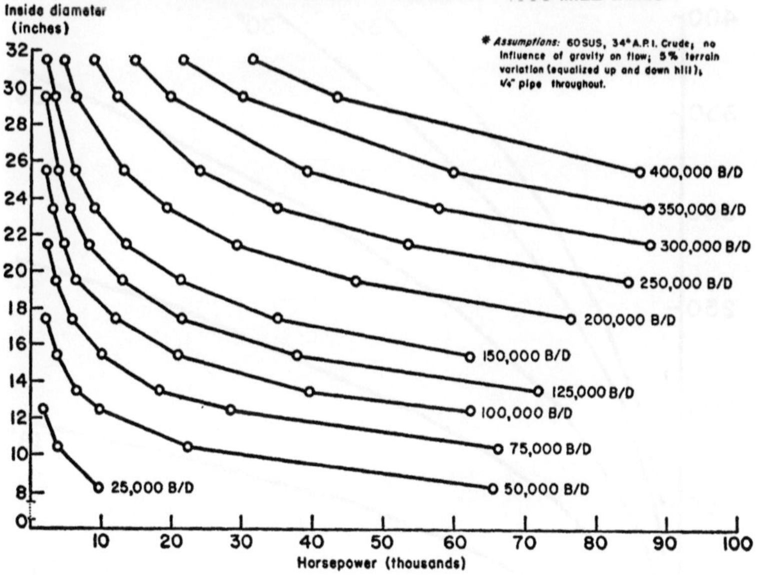

chart assumes a more or less typical Mid-Continent (60 SUS viscosity, 34° A.P.I. gravity) crude, ¼-inch pipe throughout the lines, lines 1000 miles in length with a 5 per cent terrain variation (giving 1050 miles of pipe), and no net gravity flow in the line (there may be hills as long as there are offsetting valleys). The production function covers throughputs of 25, 50, 75, 100, 125, 200, 250, 300, 350, and 400 thousand barrels per day; this encompasses the range of throughputs for crude oil trunk lines which have yet been built. The curves in the chart show the amounts of horsepower required for the several line sizes which might be used for a given throughput; each curve applies to one of the throughputs listed. The line sizes used are 8⅝, 10¾, 12¾, 14, 16, 18, 20, 22, 24, 26, 30, and 32 inches (outside

Chart 2

VERTICAL CROSS SECTION OF PRODUCTION FUNCTION: HORSEPOWER VERSUS THROUGHPUT—LINE DIAMETER HELD CONSTANT

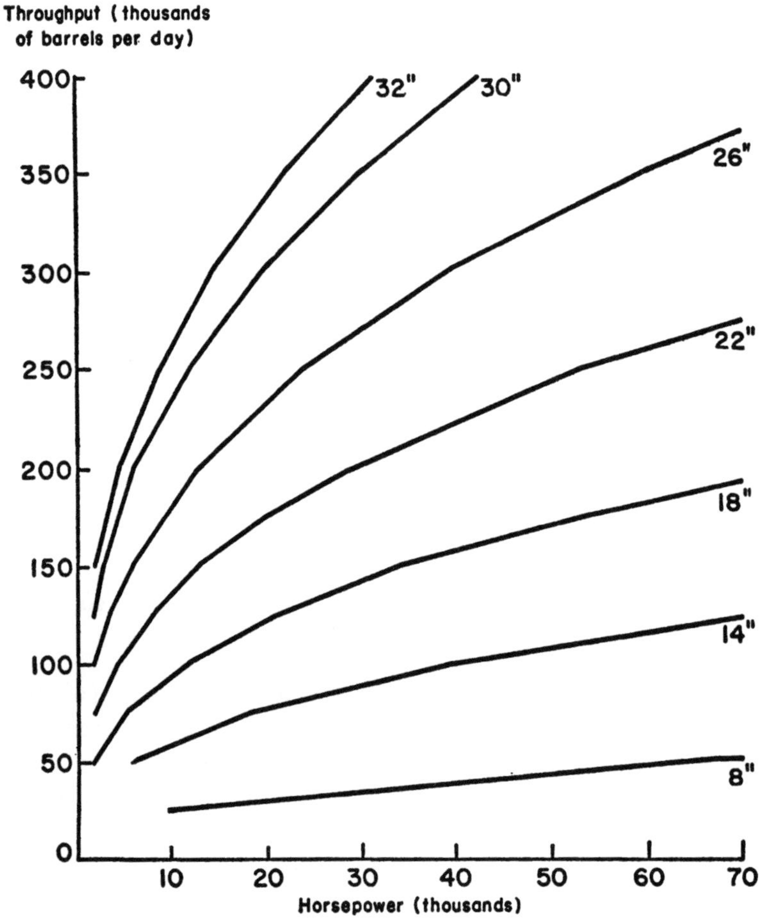

diameter) all having ¼-inch walls. This covers all line sizes used for recent crude trunk lines. (Standard line pipe is only available in these sizes in the 8–32-inch range.) It will be noted that this is in reality a three-dimensional function, with line diameter and horsepower on a plane and with the throughput axis rising perpendicularly to this plane. The production function was computed by the use of a hydraulic formula for computing required horsepowers for various volumes of liquid flow in pipes of the sizes just noted, with appropriate constants for oil of the type used. This formula, simplified, is:

$$T^{2.735} = (H)\,(D^{4.735}) \div (0.01046),$$

where,

T = Throughput,
H = Horsepower, and
D = Inside diameter of pipe.

Chart 2 shows vertical cross sections of the production function drawn perpendicular to the line-diameter axis. These are intermediate-run physical productivity curves which show the amount of horsepower that must be used with any given line size for various throughputs. They are analogous to traditional physical productivity curves of economic theory. Such a physical productivity curve in the textbooks might show the amount of wheat that can be produced from an acre of land by the use of varying numbers of workers, where line diameter is equivalent to the fixed factor (land) and horsepower is more or less equivalent to the variable factor (labor). These curves are not, however, precisely equivalent to the traditional physical productivity curves, since the horsepower factor includes some capital equipment. When it is necessary to expand output over the designed capacity of the line, it is necessary to add more capital equipment as well as more labor. When throughput is decreased below the designed capacity, unnecessary capital equipment exists — equipment on which fixed costs are incurred. Hence, as was noted above, the designation "intermediate-run" instead of short-run.

It will be observed that these productivity curves exhibit decreasing returns (marginal and average) throughout the range of throughputs. That is, there is a less than proportionate increase in throughput for a given increase in horsepower in a particular size of line. This is a physical phenomenon deriving from the characteristics of liquid flow in pipes. Other things being equal, this would mean that intermediate-run average costs attributable to horsepower should rise throughout the range of throughputs. (If the price of horsepower were constant and an addition to horsepower gave a less than proportionate increase in throughput, then the horsepower cost per barrel of throughput would rise.)

On the other hand, average costs attributable to line diameter will perforce fall throughout the range of throughputs for any given line size, since these costs are fixed in total. There are, then, offsetting forces at work, one tending to increasing average costs, the other to decreasing average costs. Whether aggregate average costs would rise, fall, or both, depends on the relative magnitudes of the horsepower and line diameter costs. In this case it will be seen that "U" shaped intermediate-run average cost curves result. That is, average costs fall at first, but then level off and rise as more and more horsepower is added to a given line. (The initial fall is accentuated by the fact that the price of horsepower falls somewhat as total horsepower used on a given line increases, thereby offsetting to some extent the decreasing physical returns.)

Chart 3 shows vertical cross sections of the production function drawn perpendicular to the horsepower axis, as opposed to those in Chart 2 which are drawn perpendicular to the line-diameter axis. These cross sections indicate what happens when horsepower is held constant and additional throughput is obtained by the use of more line-diameter (a long-run movement over the production function surface that is possible only when planning the line, not after the line is built). It will be observed that these curves exhibit *increasing* physical returns (average and marginal) to scale. This means that the same amount of horsepower applied in a large-diameter line as in a small-diameter line will give a more than proportionate increase in throughput. In other words, there is more throughput per horsepower in a large line than in a small one. Since this relationship is the basic reason for the

Chart 3

VERTICAL CROSS SECTION OF PRODUCTION FUNCTION: LINE DIAMETER VERSUS THROUGHPUT FOR SELECTED HORSEPOWERS

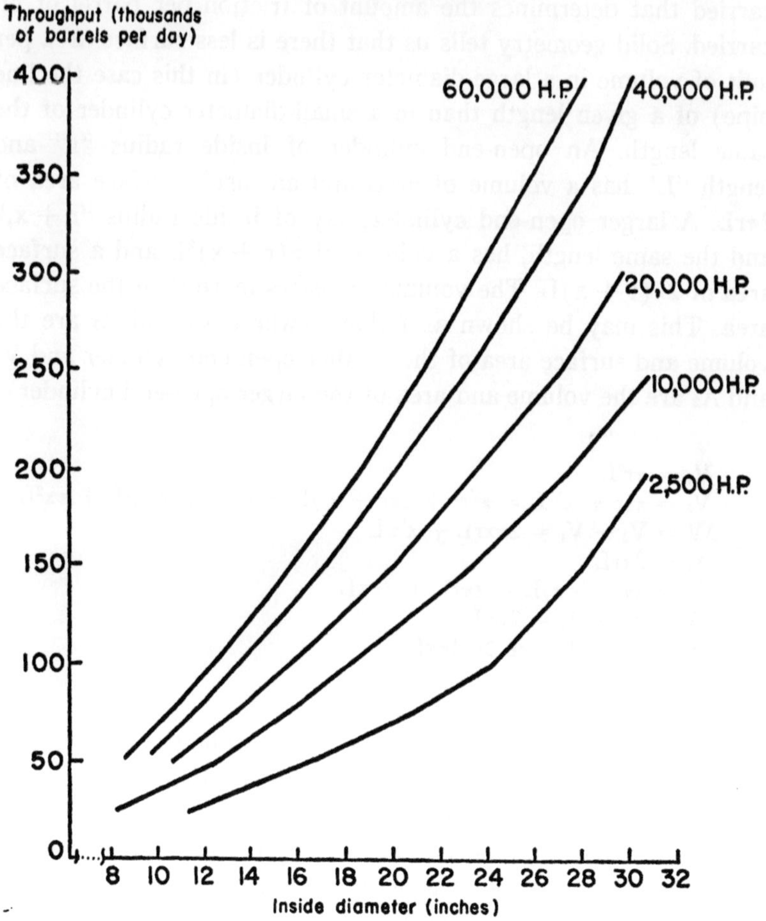

shape of the long-run cost curve, and is therefore the basis for the public policy conclusions which may be drawn from the long-run curve, it will be well to examine the physical reason for these increasing returns.

The increasing returns are attributable to the fact that there is less friction incurred per barrel of oil carried in a large-diameter pipe than in a small-diameter pipe. Friction is created by only that part of the oil which touches the inside surface of the pipe. Hence it is the amount of surface area per barrel of oil carried that determines the amount of friction per barrel of oil carried. Solid geometry tells us that there is less surface area per unit of volume in a large-diameter cylinder (in this case the line pipe) of a given length than in a small-diameter cylinder of the same length. An open-end cylinder of inside radius "r" and length "L" has a volume of $\pi r^2 L$ and an inside surface area of $2\pi rL$. A larger open-end cylinder, say of inside radius "$r + x$," and the same length, has a volume of $\pi(r + x)^2L$ and a surface area of $2\pi(r + x)L$. The volume increases more than the surface area. This may be shown as follows (where V_1 and A_1 are the volume and surface area of the smaller open-end cylinder and V_2 and A_2 are the volume and area of the larger open-end cylinder):

$$V_1 = \pi r^2 L$$
$$V_2 = \pi(r + x)^2 L = \pi(r^2 + 2xr + x^2)L = \pi r^2 L + 2\pi xrL + \pi x^2 L$$
$$\Delta V = V_2 - V_1 = 2\pi xrL + x^2\pi L$$
$$A_1 = 2\pi rL$$
$$A_2 = 2\pi(r + x)L = 2\pi rL + 2\pi xL$$
$$\Delta A = A_2 - A_1 = 2\pi xL.$$
$$\text{Since } 2\pi xrL + x^2\pi L > 2\pi xL,$$
$$\Delta V > \Delta A.$$

The volume increased by $(2\pi xrL + x^2\pi L)$, while the surface area increased only by $2\pi xL$. It may be concluded that there is more volume per unit of surface area in a large than in a small pipe. This means that more oil can be transported per unit of surface area touched in a large than a small pipe. Since the amount of friction generated depends on the amount of surface area touched, it follows that more oil can be carried per given amount of friction developed in a large than in a small pipe. Therefore, the horsepower required to overcome a given amount of friction will

Chart 4

PHYSICAL RETURNS TO SCALE. VERTICAL CROSS SECTION OF PRODUCTION FUNCTION THROUGH ORIGIN (45° ANGLE)

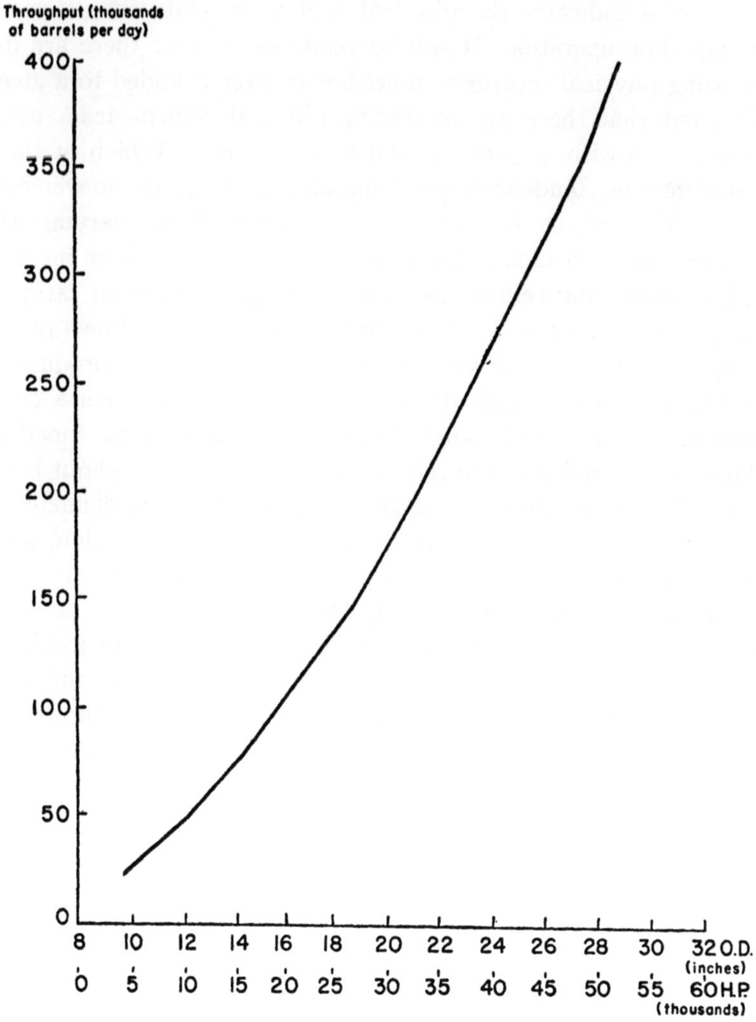

propel more oil per day through a large pipe than through a small pipe. In short, because of the volume area relationship it is possible to develop more throughput per horsepower applied in large pipes than in small ones. (It is interesting to note that the volume-area relationship is responsible for many other important technical economies of scale in industry, for example, economies of large tanks, heat containment, and so forth.)[2]

Chart 4 indicates the physical returns to scale characteristic of pipe-line operation. It will be remembered that there are decreasing physical returns as more horsepower is added to a given line, but that there are increasing physical returns from using larger lines with a given amount of horsepower. Which of these counteracting tendencies predominates in long-run movements where throughput is increased or decreased by varying the amounts of both factors used? In other words, are there increasing or decreasing returns to scale (to larger size) from carrying larger amounts of oil in the same facilities? This is shown physically by the shape of vertical cross sections of the production function drawn through the origin. Chart 4 shows such a cross section drawn at a 45° angle through the origin of the function. This section indicates the returns to scale when throughput is increased by increasing the use of horsepower and line diameter in equal proportions. (Note that this is only an approximation, since the production function is only realistic at certain points, not over its whole surface; consequently, the 45° line would only by chance intersect each throughput at a point where an available line size exists.) The curve exhibits increasing (average and marginal) returns to scale throughout the range of throughputs. In other words, if the amounts of horsepower and line diameter used are increased in equal proportions, then there would be a more than proportionate increase in throughput. This indicates that on an a priori basis it would be expected that long-run decreasing average costs would characterize pipe-line operation. Only if the

[2] See H. B. Chenerey, Engineering Bases of Economic Analysis, unpublished doctoral thesis deposited in Widener Library (1950), pp. 140–141, and E. A. G. Robinson, *Structure of Competitive Industry* (London, 1935), p. 29.

price of one or both of the factors should increase sufficiently with the amount of the factor used to offset the increasing returns, would the long-run cost curve turn up. Actually, the price of horsepower decreases somewhat with the amount used, and the price of line diameter does not fluctuate sufficiently with the amount used to offset the physical relationship.

Lest the reader object to drawing these general conclusions only on the basis of an example where expansion is by increased utilization of the factors in equal proportions, it should be pointed out that this is a "homogeneous" production function. Homogeneous production functions exhibit the same type of returns to scale on all parts of the surface. The function used reduces to (see page 17):

$$T^{2.735} = (H)(D^{4.735})(C), \quad \text{or}$$

$$T = (H^{\frac{1}{2.735}})(D^{\frac{4.735}{2.735}})(C) = (H^{.37})(D^{1.73})(C).$$

This is a function of the form,

$$T = H^m D^n C.$$

Such a function is homogeneous if $(m + n)$ is a constant, as it is in this case, where $(m + n) = 2.1$. This also indicates that there are marked increasing returns to scale, since the function is of order 2 (constant returns to scale are implied from a function having an order of one).

The discussion of the technological relationships peculiar to pipe-line transportation of oil may now be summarized. A basic physical relationship may be deduced for the purpose of computing pipe-line costs. This relationship shows that there will be markedly increasing long-run physical returns to scale if larger and larger throughputs are carried. In the intermediate-run physical returns decrease. It follows, assuming that factor prices are more or less constant with the amount of the factor used, that there will be long-run decreasing costs (economies of scale) for pipe-line operation. Intermediate-run costs might rise, fall, or both—since the increasing average costs attributable to horsepower are counteracted by fixed costs attributable to line diameter. Under such conditions, "U"-shaped curves are feasible. These cost conclusions are based solely on the physical relationships discussed and are independent of the cost determination to be considered next. The conclusions would be invalidated only if the price of one or both of the factors rose sufficiently with increases in the amount of the factor used to offset the increasing physical returns to scale. This is not the case. (This may also be predicted to a considerable extent apart from actual cost determination, since the amounts of the most important single cost items included in each factor are proportional to the amounts of the factors used.)

Costs. — Pipe-line costs may be divided into three basic categories: (1) those variant with line diameter; (2) those variant with horsepower; (3) those variant only with throughput or length of line (a relatively small part of total cost). Since there is a choice for any given throughput among several possible combinations of line diameter and horsepower (as is shown in the production function in Chart 1), in order to be able to compute a long-run cost curve it is necessary to determine which of several possible combinations is least expensive for any throughput. This is done for each throughput by determining the total cost of each possible combination, on, say, an annual basis. That combination whose total cost is least for a given throughput is the optimum combination for that throughput. Note that it is only the costs of line diameter and horsepower which must be so manipulated, since the other costs are irrelevant to the choice of the optimum combination of these two. The other costs are, of course, incurred and cannot be ignored; but they do not influence the choice of the proper size line for a given throughput.

Annual total intermediate-run costs are shown in Chart 5; these are derived by plotting annual total cost against throughput for each line diameter covered in the study. The shaded envelope of the intermediate-run cost curves is the long-run total cost curve. Chart 6 shows intermediate-run costs per barrel per 1000 miles (that is, average costs). This is a chart analogous to Figure 1 above. Its envelope is the long-run average cost curve. In the range of throughputs where the average cost curve of a given line size lies below all other average cost curves, that line is the optimum line for the throughputs covered. For example, the 30-inch line lies beneath all others between about 225,000

Chart 5

ANNUAL TOTAL COSTS OF OPERATING CRUDE OIL TRUNK PIPE LINES

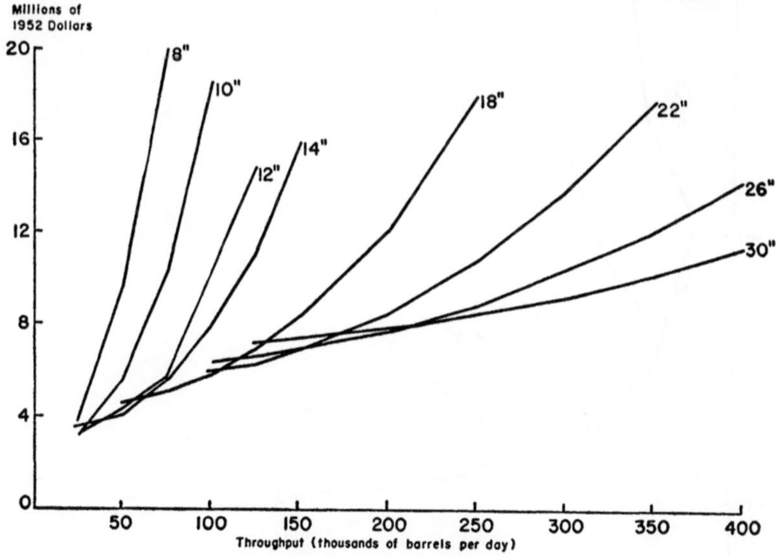

Source: L. Cookenboo, Jr., "Costs of Operating Crude Oil Pipe Lines," *Rice Institute Pamphlet,* April 1954, pp. 106–107 (Table 19).

and 325,000 barrels per day; hence, it is the optimum line for throughputs between those limits.

The intermediate-run cost curves also show what it would cost to carry larger quantities of oil than the design throughput if stations were added subsequent to the building of the line. (Pipe lines cannot be operated at throughputs greater than the designed capacity without the additions of more stations, since the design capacity would require the highest operating pressures permitted by the safety factor.) Remember that the intermediate-run curve does *not* show the costs of throughputs less than the design throughput.

Chart 6

COSTS PER BARREL OF OPERATING CRUDE OIL TRUNK PIPE LINES

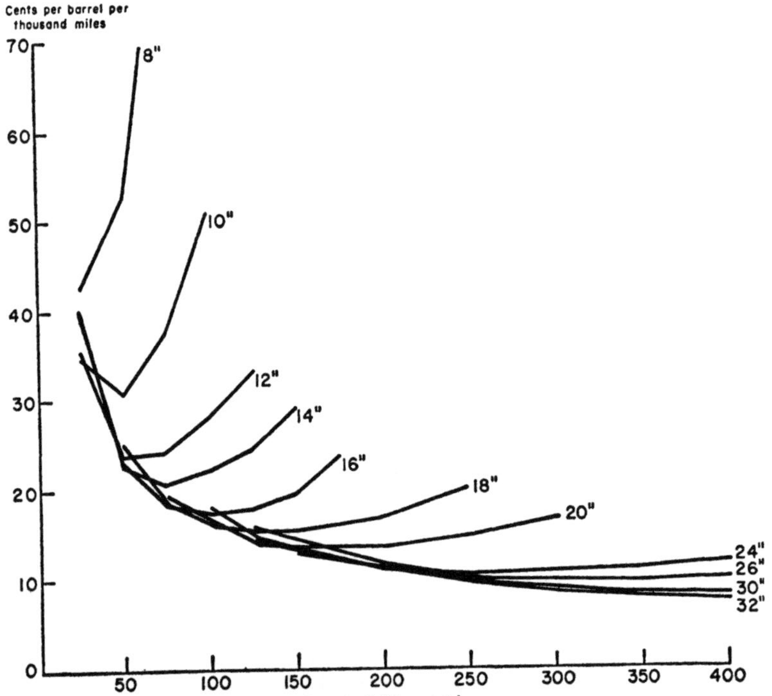

Source: L. Cookenboo, Jr., "Costs of Operating Crude Oil Pipe Lines," *Rice Institute Pamphlet,* April 1954, pp. 106–107 (Table 19).

While, as was pointed out above, the details of the cost study lying behind the totals in Charts 5 and 6 and discussed at length elsewhere,[3] a word or two should be said about the assumptions involved in the engineering-type cost determination. The principal

[3] Cookenboo, "Costs of Operating Crude Oil Pipe Lines," pp. 35–113.

items involved in the cost of line diameter are all represented by initial outlays made during the construction of the line. The most important line costs are the service costs of laying the line, and the material costs of steel, pipe coating, line block valves, corrosion protection, and so forth. The assumptions of the characteristics of the lines, listed above, were 1000 miles of ¼-inch pipe having 50 miles of terrain variation (with no net gravity flow). This means that the line costs include the material and service costs of laying 1050 miles of pipe (coated in accord with the best coating practice and protected by magnesium anodes).

The principal items involved in the costs of horsepower are the annual expenditures for electric power and labor (and of less importance, maintenance) to operate the pumping stations. This category also includes the initial cost of the stations; this represents the most difficult, time-consuming part of a pipe-line cost computation (even though station costs are not too important in relation to total costs). The stations used on the pipe lines described in Charts 5 and 6 are semiautomatic, equipped with centrifugal pumps and electric motors. Stations pumping over 100,000 barrels per day are equipped with three full-size pumps and motors (one motor per pump) which together deliver the capacity throughput, and one half-size pump and motor. This provides flexibility of operation which would otherwise be unattainable with constant speed electric motors. (With, as they say, 3½ pumps, seven stages of operation are possible: no pumps, ½ pump, 1½, 2, 2½, and 3 for capacity.) Stations pumping less than 100,000 barrels per day utilize two full-size pumps and one half-size pump. Each station utilizes in-and-out piping to permit the bypassing of any one pump without shutting down the whole station. The labor force required for such semiautomatic stations is two men per shift (regardless of the level of operation), unless the stations are very large; none used in this study was large enough to require extra operators. (In a semiautomatic pumping station the principal tasks of the operators are to watch the controls, shut off motor-operated valves when necessary, and maintain the equipment.)

The principal costs involved in the "other" category are the initial costs of (1) tankage (the lines in this study have 12.5 days' supply of storage capacity along the line), (2) surveying the right-of-way, (3) damages to terrain crossed, and (4) a communications system (here assumed to be a 12-channel microwave system). It should be noted that while these costs vary either with throughput or with length of line, they are *proportional* to either throughput or length of line as the case may be. There are no significant per-barrel costs of a pipe line which change with length. The only such costs are those of a central office force; these are inconsequential in relation to total. Hence, it is possible to state that costs per barrel-mile for a 1000-mile trunk line are representative of costs per barrel-mile of any trunk line (those, say, 75 or 100 miles in length and longer).

It will be observed in Chart 6 that there are economies of scale (decreasing long-run average costs) throughout the range of throughputs covered. The analysis was only carried through 32-inch lines and 400,000 barrels per day. However, if larger lines could be had at a constant price per ton of steel (the only price per unit of material likely to change with larger amounts than those used), then the long-run average cost curve would fall even farther. On the other hand, pipe much larger than 34 or 36 inches might well require the creation of special pipe-making facilities and, consequently, might command a higher price per ton than the pipe sizes used in this study. In this case, the long-run average cost curve might turn up near, say, 500,000 barrels per day. In any event, the rate of decrease of the average cost curve has declined appreciably by the time a throughput of 400,000 barrels per day is reached. Consequently, the cost per barrel of carrying a throughput of 400,000 barrels per day is probably close to the minimum that can be achieved with present pipe-making facilities.

It may also be noted from Chart 6, especially in the case of the large-diameter lines, that throughput can be expanded appreciably over the design throughput before higher per-barrel costs than the original costs are incurred. (For a while, of course, there would actually be a decline in per-barrel costs.) For example, a 24-inch line built for 200,000 barrels per day could, if necessary, later be used for 300,000 barrels per day (after adding the required number of stations) without incurring increased costs per barrel.

Chart 7

SHORT-RUN AVERAGE COSTS OF TRANSPORTING CRUDE OIL IN TRUNK LINES

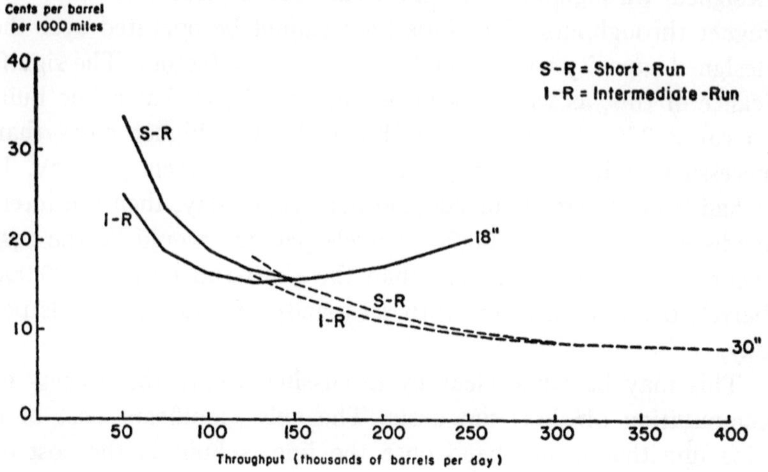

Note: Eighteen-in. line designed for 150,000 barrels per day. Thirty-in. line designed for 300,000 barrels per day.

Short-run cost curves could be computed for any of the possible combinations of line diameter and horsepower shown in Chart 1 — since each line would have a different short-run cost curve for each throughput it might carry. Building seven stations on an 18-inch line would yield one short-run curve. Building ten stations on an 18-inch line would yield another short-run curve. Building seven stations on a 20-inch line would yield yet another short-run curve — ad infinitum. To avoid the labor involved in computing short-run costs for every combination of line diameter and horsepower covered in the study (75 in all), two were computed: one for an 18-inch line carrying 100,000 barrels per day, another for a 30-inch line carrying 300,000 barrels per day. The relative positions of short- and intermediate-run curves would be the same for any other combinations of line diameter and horsepower. These short-run average cost curves are shown in Chart 7.

Observe that short-run average costs are always higher than intermediate-run average costs for throughputs less than the designed throughput (the short-run curve does not exist for higher throughputs, since pipe lines cannot be operated over the designed capacity without violating the safety factor). The significance of this, as will be seen in Chapter IV, is that a line built to carry 250,000 barrels per day will incur higher costs than necessary if it consistently carries 200,000 barrels per day. If it had been designed for 200,000 barrels per day, then the intermediate-run cost for 200,000 barrels per day would be the cost incurred. This figure is less than the short-run cost of 200,000 barrels per day on a line with a capacity of 250,000 barrels per day.

This may be made clear by discussing briefly the process of computation of short-run costs. The only significant cost of a pipe line that is not fixed once the line is built is the cost of electric power. If the line is run below capacity, as many workers are still needed; and, of course, the same number of stations and the same amount of pipe exists. The only significant saving is in power costs. In order to compute short-run costs one simply subtracts the cost of the appropriate amount of electric power which is saved when throughput is cut to various levels from the intermediate-run cost at the designed output. This figure must be higher than intermediate-run costs of lesser throughputs because these costs are computed upon the basis of the proper (smaller) number of stations for the smaller throughputs. It should be noted that a given cut in throughput means a more than proportionate saving in power requirements, since electric power requirements vary with horsepower requirements. Remember that it takes a more than proportionate increase in horsepower to get a given increase in throughput; conversely, a decrease in throughput means a more than proportionate decrease in horsepower required — and hence a more than proportionate decrease in electric power required.

Summary. — Intermediate-, long-, and short-run costs for carrying crude oil were computed.

The long- and intermediate-run cost curves computed in a study of the engineering estimation type are of the same shape that would be predicted from the physical production functions for pipe-line transportation of crude (with no consideration of costs). The physical production function is homogeneous of order 2; under these conditions there will be marked economies of scale unless factor prices rise sharply with the amount of the factor used. This is not the case in the range of throughputs and line sizes covered.

The long-run average cost curve falls throughout the range of throughputs covered (see Chart 6), and it would continue to fall indefinitely if larger pipe could be obtained without paying a premium price. However, the rate of decline of long-run costs per barrel has slowed considerably by the time a throughput of 400,000 barrels per day is reached. Intermediate-run curves are "U" shaped, but throughput can be increased appreciably over the designed level without increased per-barrel costs — especially in the case of large-diameter lines where the "U" is rather flat over wide ranges of throughputs.

Short-run costs are always greater than intermediate-run costs for a given line size. The only significant variable cost in pipe-line operation is the cost of power (or fuel).

It may be concluded from these cost curves that the economies of scale characteristic of the operation of pipe lines require that oil must be carried conglomerately in as large quantities as is possible in large-diameter line. This gives the least transportation costs obtainable — the optimum situation from the point of view of both the firm and society. Furthermore, pipe lines should not be run at throughputs appreciably below capacity; otherwise higher (short-run) costs per barrel will be incurred than need be. Finally, the capacity of a large line can be expanded appreciably without increasing average costs; indeed, *decreased* average costs can be obtained with moderate expansions.

II

PETROLEUM INDUSTRY STRUCTURE*

In this chapter an investigation will be made of the structure of the crude oil pipe-line stage of the industry and of the refining and producing stages insofar as this is necessary.

As was noted in the introduction, the major oil companies are asserted to have dominated crude oil pipe lines and to have used this domination to control the rest of the industry. The question at hand is the extent of this domination, both past and current. In the succeeding section of the chapter the relationship of major domination of crude pipe lines and the locational structure of the refining stage of the industry will be discussed. Finally, the relationship of the size of crude producing areas to pipe-line size will be investigated in Section C.

Before proceeding it is necessary to specify more precisely what is meant by a "major" oil company. The problem of "major" versus "independent" arises almost always during discussions where the major is a large, integrated company and the independent is a smaller (oppressed) company. The extent of smallness necessary to qualify as an oppressed instead of an oppressing company is not clear. However, those companies generally designated as majors are the first fifteen or twenty in terms of total assets. These have been assigned to the "major" category; subsequently in the inquiry this definition will be modified somewhat.

The following companies are included in subsequent tabulations as "majors": Standard (New Jersey), Standard (Indiana), Texas Company, Socony-Vacuum, Gulf, Shell, Sinclair, Standard of California, Phillips, Cities Service, Atlantic Refining, Union,

* Statistics were tabulated principally in late 1952 and 1953; hence some estimates made then may not agree precisely with actual data. Any differences cannot be important enough to affect conclusions.

TABLE 1

Cumulative Percentages of Total Crude Throughput

	1940		
Company	No. of Companies	Cumulative Total (000,000 bbls.)	Cumulative % of U.S.
Standard (N.J.)	1	224.3	13.4
Texas Co.		176.5	10.6
	2	400.8	24.0
Socony		131.9	7.9
	3	532.7	31.9
Standard (Ind.)		92.6	5.5
	4	625.3	37.4
Ohio Oil Co.		90.4	5.4
	5	715.7	42.8
Standard (Calif.)		82.6	4.9
	6	798.3	47.7
Gulf		78.1	4.7
	7	876.4	52.4
Cities Service		73.6	4.4
	8	950.0	56.8
Sinclair		71.7	4.3
	9	1021.7	61.1
Phillips		60.1	3.6
	10	1081.8	64.7
Atlantic		56.4	3.4
	11	1138.2	68.1
Shell		52.0	3.1
	12	1190.2	71.2
Pure		50.5	3.0
	13	1240.7	74.2
Union		45.6	2.7
	14	1286.3	76.9
Continental		36.9	2.2
	15	1323.2	69.1
Tide Water		29.2	1.7
	16	1352.4	80.8
Standard (Ohio)		28.9	1.7
	17	1381.3	82.5
Sun Oil Co.		22.3	1.3
	18	1403.6	83.8
Skelly		10.0	0.6
	19	1413.6	84.5[a]

[a] Detail does not necessarily add to total due to rounding.

Source: Company data from Moody's *Industrials*, TNEC *Hearings* (XIV-A), Justice Department Questionnaire, *Annual Reports*, Trade Journal articles, SEC Form 10-K Reports, and private sources. Totals estimated.

in Pipe Lines — Nineteen Major Oil Companies

	1948		
Company	No. of Companies	Cumulative Total (000,000 bbls.)	Cumulative % of U.S.
Standard (N.J.)	1	598.2	19.1
Texas Co.		239.5	7.6
	2	837.7	26.7
Standard (Ind.)		216.8	6.9
	3	1054.5	33.6
Socony		200.3	6.4
	4	1254.8	40.0
Gulf		186.0	5.9
	5	1440.8	45.9
Shell		176.6	5.6
	6	1617.4	51.5
Standard (Calif.)		165.2	5.2
	7	1782.6	56.7
Sinclair		147.1	4.7
	8	1929.7	61.4
Ohio Oil Co.		132.4	4.2
	9	2062.1	65.6
Atlantic		120.4	3.8
	10	2182.5	69.4
Cities Service		99.6	3.2
	11	2282.1	72.6
Phillips		93.3	3.0
	12	2375.4	75.6
Sun Oil Co.		77.2	2.4
	13	2452.6	78.0
Standard (Ohio)		76.5	2.4
	14	2529.1	80.4
Union		72.8	2.3
	15	2601.9	82.7
Continental		63.3	2.0
	16	2665.2	84.7
Pure		53.9	1.7
	17	2719.1	86.4
Tide Water		32.2	1.0
	18	2751.3	87.4
Skelly		28.8	0.9
	19	2780.1	88.2[a]

Tide Water, Standard (Ohio), Continental, Sun, Pure, and the Ohio Oil Company. Skelly must also be included, even though it is small, since it is allied with Tide Water in the Getty group of companies. In addition, Richfield should probably be included since it is jointly controlled by Sinclair and Cities Service; however, since the actual extent of its subservience to these companies is unknown, it will be omitted from the following tabulations of majors. Its addition would add one or two percentage points to the majors' share of the market.

A. PIPE LINES

Two separate measures of the role of the major oil companies in crude oil pipe lines have been made. The first is shown in Table 1. This table shows the share of total crude throughput held by each of the nineteen major companies in 1940 and 1948. This covers both oil carried in trunk lines and in field-gathering systems. Total throughput was determined for each year by adding to the total reported by the Interstate Commerce Commission for interstate lines the reported totals of all other companies for which data were available in published sources (company annual reports, Moody's *Industrials,* stock exchange prospectuses, SEC form 10 K's, Congressional hearings, trade journal articles, and others). As a result, it must be pointed out that these data tend to overstate the position of the major companies, since data were more readily available for them. However, any error from this source could not be unduly large.

In addition, there is double counting in the figures in that the same oil carried by two connecting lines often appears twice. The effect of this on the relative positions of majors and independents is not readily predictable, since it depends on what the proper measure of concentration is in this stage of the industry. If it be the relationship of each company's barrels per day of throughput to total barrels per day carried, then the double counting would most likely overstate the position of the majors, since independents' gathering systems would not be counted twice. On the other hand, if the proper measure of concentration be in terms of barrel-*miles*, not simply barrels, then oil carried farther should be given heavier weight. Indeed, the computation should be made in terms of barrel-miles. Such data are, however, not available for all companies. It should be noted that the use of pipe-line *mileage* alone is unacceptable. A company which owns a thousand miles of 8-inch line carrying 30,000 barrels per day is clearly not the equal of a company which owns a thousand miles of 30-inch line carrying 300,000 barrels per day.

What *is* the proper measure of concentration in pipe lines? At first glance it might seem that barrels per day carried in lines owned by majors (with double counting eliminated) in relation to total barrels carried is correct for a general economy-wide statement of the position of the majors. Furthermore, the use of barrel-miles on a nation-wide basis gives erroneous impressions. For example, assume that there are only two refineries, one an independent refinery located at a market 300 miles from its source of supply; this company owns a 10,000-barrel-per-day line — giving it 3,000,000 barrel-miles per day of capacity. The other company is a major having a 50,000-barrel-per-day line carrying oil 1000 miles to its refinery at some other market — giving it 50,000,000 barrel-miles per day of capacity. Using barrel-miles as the measure of concentration, the major would be found to have 50/53 of the market (94 per cent). Using barrels per day it would have 50/60 (83 per cent). Does it really not have 83 per cent, since it only accounts for 5/6 of the oil carried in pipe lines, not 94 per cent?

The answer is that it has neither 94 per cent nor 83 per cent of the "market." It is simply not possible to make any precise, meaningful statements about nation-wide shares of the market in a transportation industry. The important factor insofar as market control is concerned is what percentage of total pipe-line capacity *between a given producing area and a given refining center* is owned by one, two, three, or more companies. It is of little concern to an independent refiner on the Gulf Coast whether pipe lines from West Texas to Chicago are owned by majors, other independents, or the government. However, the ownership of lines from West Texas to the Gulf Coast may well be of intimate concern to him. Such statements as, "The majors have 90 per cent of pipe line capacity; therefore independent refiners can be largely controlled by the majors," really do not mean very much. What matters is the ownership of pipe lines between given producing areas and given refining areas. Note, however, that if the percentage is 100, the statement is true. On the other hand, while the immediate presumption would be that the statement is true if the percentage is very high, say 97.5 per cent, it should become clear in Section B that this is not necessarily the case.

In any event, Table 1 shows that the major companies owned lines which carried 84.5 per cent of crude shipped in pipe lines in 1940 and 88.2 per cent in 1948. A similar computation made on the basis of inter-state shipments alone showed about 80 per cent in 1929. The years 1940 and 1948 were chosen to describe the situation before and after World War II (1948 was used as the postwar year because it was a year of almost capacity operation for nearly all companies). Data for the mid-thirties quoted in the TNEC proceedings showed, using the defective mileage basis for computation, that twenty majors owned 95.4 per cent of trunk lines in 1936 and about 89 per cent in 1938.[1] (Mileage was not quite so defective a measure then as it would be now, since there were no large-diameter lines.)

Even though only five years have passed, the 1948 data (aside from their other imperfections) are not acceptable for the current structure of the crude oil pipe-line stage of the industry. Since World War II there has been a major change in the building of crude oil trunk lines, namely, the introduction of large-diameter, mass-transportation lines. Only a few of these lines had been completed by 1948; the rest have been built and put into operation since that date, or are still under construction. The principal new interregional crude lines, which will be discussed further in the last chapter of the study, are shown in

[1] TNEC *Hearings,* Part 14A, p. 7723.

Table 2. These lines have an aggregate capacity of about 1.5 million barrel-miles per day, compared with a total interregional system capacity of about 2.5 million barrel-miles per day.

What are the relative positions of the large and small companies in the ownership of the new lines on a local basis and in the economy as a whole? The answer, as one might anticipate, is that the major companies own nearly all the new, more efficient lines. Indeed, only four other oil companies have any holdings in the lines which carry United States crude (the two systems originating in Canada will be discussed later). These four companies are British-American (a Canadian company), Eastern States, Republic, and Crown-Central. The last three companies are independent refineries which own shares in the Rancho system from West Texas to the Gulf Coast. Republic is in reality part of an integrated company, since it is a subsidiary of the important independent producer, Plymouth (controlled by the Benedum interests), which has large holdings in Texas.

British-American owns a 20 per cent share in the line from Portland (Maine) to Montreal (amounting to 25,400 barrels per day) and a 15 per cent share in the Platte system (some 13,500 barrels per day). The three Gulf Coast refiners own a total of 15 per cent of the Rancho system (about 31,400 barrels per day). This is about 2 per cent of total trunk-line capacity from West Texas to the middle Gulf Coast (the other two systems constitute their own local markets). In order to draw a general picture of the relative economy-wide importance of majors and independents, the share of barrel-mile capacity of the lines is also shown in Table 2. The majors own 97.5 per cent of this capacity, while 1.5 per cent is owned by the Canadian company and a university and 1.0 per cent is owned by three United States independent refiners.

The two pipe lines originating in the Alberta field in Canada (one going east, the other west) are owned by majors, independent producers and refiners, and outside interests. The relative shares are not readily determinable, since more stock is being

TABLE 2

Size and Ownership of Principal Interregional Crude Oil Trunk Lines Built Since 1944 to Carry United States Crude

Line and Location	Approx. Completion Date	Outside Diameter	Length	Approximate Capacity Barrels Per Day	Approximate Capacity Barrel-Miles Per Day	Ownership Majors	Ownership Others	Company Ownership
		(inches)	(miles)	000's	000's	per cent	per cent	
(1) Magnolia W. Texas-E. Texas	1944	12¾	337	40	13,500	100	—	Socony
(2) Stanolind W. Texas-Okla.	1944	16	385	65	25,000	100	—	Stand. (Ind.)
(3) Stand. of Calif.	1947	18	176	125	22,000	100	—	Stand. (Calif.)
(4) Magnolia E. Texas-Illinois	1947	20	647	100	64,700	100	—	Socony
(5) Salt Lake Rangely Colo.-Salt Lake City	1948	10¾	182	20	3,600	100	—	Socony
(6) Basin W. Texas-Okla.	1949	20, 22, 24	516	358	184,700[a]	100	—	Joint Venture
(7) Ozark Okla.-Ill. (Wood River)	1949	22	433	283	122,500	100	—	Joint Venture
(8) Texas-Empire S. Ill.-Chicago	1949	18	181	73	13,200	100	—	Joint Venture
(9) Portland Portland, Me.-Montreal	1949	18	236	127	30,000	80	20	Joint Venture
(10) Humble W. Texas-Gulf Coast	1950	18	370	135	50,000	100	—	Stand. (N.J.)
(11) Atlantic W. Texas-S. Gulf Coast	1950	10¾	383	46	17,600	100	—	Atlantic
(12) Mid-Valley E. Texas-Ohio	1952	20, 22	933	235	219,300[a]	100	—	Joint Venture
(13) Paso-Tex. W. Texas-El Paso	1952	8	195	12	2,300	100	—	Stand. (Calif.)
(14) Continental S. Texas-Gulf Coast	1952	8	105	17	1,800	50	50	Joint Venture
(15) Continental N. Texas-Okla.	1952	12	127	40	5,000	100	—	Continental
(16) Phillips W. Texas-Okla.	1952	10	280	23	6,400	100	—	Phillips
(17) Sinclair Okla.-Chicago (via Wood River)	1952	22, 24	675	280	189,000[a]	100	—	Sinclair
(18) Platte Wyo.-(Ill.) (Wood River)	1952	20	1,080	100	108,000	85	15	Joint Venture

TABLE 2 (Continued)

Line and Location	Approx. Completion Date	Outside Diameter	Length	Approximate Capacity Barrels Per Day	Approximate Capacity Barrel-Miles Per Day	Ownership Majors	Ownership Others	Company Ownership
		(inches)	(miles)	000's	000's	per cent	per cent	
(19) Ohio Ill. (Wood River)-Ohio	1952	22	362	180	65,100	100	—	Ohio
(20) West Tex. Gulf W. Tex.-E. Tex.-Gulf Coast (Tex.)	1953	20, 26	660	381	229,800[a]	100	—	Joint Venture
(21) Cities Service Tex. Gulf Coast-Lake Charles, La.	1953	18	64	150	9,600	100	—	Cities Service
(22) Rancho W. Tex.-Gulf Coast	1953	24	463	209	96,800	85	15	Joint Venture
(23) Texas Co. La. Gulf Coast-Tex. Gulf Coast	1953	22	220	175	38,500	100	—	Texas Co.
(24) Texas Co. E. Texas-Gulf Coast	1953	16	187	60	11,200	100	—	Texas Co.
(25) Humble E. Texas-Gulf Coast	1954	12, 18	201	66	13,300[a]	100	—	Stand. (N. J.)
Total U.S.		22[b]	9,398	3,300	1,542,900	97.5 [b]	2.5[b]	

[a] More than one line size, barrels times miles may not equal barrel-miles, since only one throughput is shown for each line.
[b] Weighted by barrel-miles.
General Notes: The following combinations of lines make up systems: (a) (6), (7), and (8); (b) (20), (12), and (13); (c) (18) and (19).

Joint Venture Ownership

(6) Basin — Texaco, 45 per cent; Shell, 35 per cent; Sinclair, 11 per cent; Cities Service, 9 per cent.
(7) Ozark — Texaco, 45 per cent; Shell, 55 per cent.
(8) Texas Empire — Texaco, 50 per cent; Cities Service, 50 per cent.
(9) Portland-Montreal — Stand. (N.J.), 40 per cent; Texaco, 20 per cent; Shell, 20 per cent; British-American, 20 per cent.
(12) Mid-Valley — Stand. (Ohio), 50 per cent; Sun, 50 per cent.
(14) Continental — Continental, 50 per cent; others, 50 per cent.
(18) Phillips — Sinclair, 25 per cent; Pure, 15 per cent; Continental, 20 per cent; Ohio, 25 per cent; British-American, 15 per cent.
(20) West Texas Gulf — Gulf, 57 per cent; Cities Service, 11 per cent; Stand. (Ohio), 10 per cent; Sun, 13 per cent.
(22) Rancho — Shell, 38 per cent; Sinclair, 20 per cent; Stand. (Ind.) 21 per cent; Phillips, 6 per cent; 3 independents, 15 per cent.

Source: Assembled from information in various trade journal construction reports, company annual reports, stock exchange prospectuses, Moody's *Industrials*, and private sources.

sold to the public. However, the original shares in Trans-Mountain (to the Pacific Northwest) were as shown in the accompanying table.

Interprovincial (and its extension Lakehead) to Lake Superior and Ontario was originated by Imperial (a Jersey subsidiary). This company originally held about one-third of the line; other

Original Ownership of Trans-Mountain Pipe Line Company

	Shares (000's)	Per Cent of Total
Standard (N.J.)	130	8⅔
Standard of Calif.	130	8⅔
Gulf	130	8⅔
Shell	130	8⅔
Union	100	6⅔
Richfield	50	3⅓
Independents	250	16⅔
Bechtel[a]	130	8⅔
Public	450	30
Total	1,500	100

[a] Bechtel is a large construction company which built and will operate the line.
Source: Shares held from G. M. Wilson, "Alberta Crude to Head West," *World Oil*, September 1952, pp. 303–304.

oil companies held 25 per cent; and a few outsiders held 42 per cent (total stockholders, 18).[2] Stock is now being sold on the market, and Jersey's share had fallen to 24 per cent as of its 1953 annual report.

Summary. — To the extent possible the role of the majors in crude pipe-line ownership has been quantified, with an indication that some 85 per cent of crude throughput in the United States was in lines owned by the large companies before the change in trunk-line construction. In the case of the new large-diameter lines, the majors have complete control in all areas except for the small shares owned by a Canadian company and by three Gulf Coast independent refiners in the West Texas–Gulf Coast capac-

[2] See Moody's *Industrials* and annual reports of Standard (N.J.) and Interprovincial.

ity. On the other hand, the two new Canadian systems, while principally owned by the interested major companies, are also owned by independent refiners, independent producers, and the public.

Crude oil trunk lines, then, are owned primarily by the major oil companies, as has been repeatedly asserted throughout the period of controversy over the effect of such ownership. However, this in itself does not necessarily mean that the major companies thereby dominate existing independents in other stages of the industry, specifically in refining and production. Simply being an independent refiner does not automatically make one a part of the market for the services of the crude trunk lines, that is, the refining market. What is the extent of this market? Where is it situated geographically? What is the relative importance of majors and independents in refining?

B. REFINING

It is now necessary to inquire into the size of refineries, refining companies, and refining areas. This inquiry has two principal purposes: (1) to determine the extent to which the economies of scale discussed in the preceding chapter may be achieved in oil transportation, and (2) to evaluate the competitive role of the various independent refiners.

The economy-wide position of the nineteen major companies in the refining stage of the industry is shown in Table 3. The measure used is physical input of crude petroleum to the refineries ("runs to stills") in terms of average barrels per day for the years 1929, 1937, 1948, and 1952. The total accounted for by all of these companies in relation to total United States runs is shown for all intervening years in Chart 8. Chart 9 shows cumulative percentages held by the companies ranked by size for the years 1930 and 1952. The percentage of the market accounted for by these companies is amazingly stable; indeed, the small variations may well not be significant when potential errors in the reporting systems are considered.

A nation-wide picture is not, however, sufficient. The effect of

TABLE 3

Runs to Stills of Nineteen Major Oil Companies, 1930, 1937, 1948, 1952

Company	1930 Runs (000,000 Barrels)	1930 % of U.S. Total	1930 Rank	1937 Runs (000,000 Barrels)	1937 % of U.S. Total	1937 Rank	1948 Runs (000,000 Barrels)	1948 % of U.S. Total	1948 Rank	1952 Runs (000,000 Barrels)	1952 % of U.S. Total	1952 Rank
Standard (N.J.)	132.8	14.4	1	144.0	12.2	1	272.2	13.4	1	285.1	11.7	1
Socony-Vacuum	75.6	8.2	2	100.6	8.5	2	172.6	8.5	2	185.7	7.6	3
Gulf	67.7	7.3	3	77.9	6.6	6	140.6	6.9	5	166.1	6.8	5
Shell	67.2	7.3	4	84.5	7.1	5	116.3	5.7	6	139.8	5.7	7
Standard (Ind.)	58.9	6.4	5	87.0	7.4	4	156.2	7.7	3	185.3	7.6	4
Texas Co.	57.4	6.2	6	96.3	8.1	3	146.0	7.2	4	192.2	7.9	2
Standard (Cal.)	52.0	5.6	7	53.8	4.5	8	112.4	5.5	7	149.4	6.1	6
Tide Water	41.2	4.5	8	44.0	3.7	9	59.8	2.9	11	54.9	2.2	13
Sinclair	36.4	3.9	9	65.0	5.5	7	94.6	4.7	8	132.3	5.4	8
Union	28.2	3.1	10	26.3	2.2	13	41.0	2.0	14	49.8	2.0	14
Atlantic	26.0	2.8	11	35.3	3.0	10	53.8	2.6	12	64.8	2.7	12
Cities Service	18.9	2.0	12	33.3	2.8	11	72.6	3.6	9	86.8	3.6	9
Pure	17.7	1.9	13	28.6	2.4	12	38.3	1.9	15	37.4	1.5	16
Sun	16.0	1.7	14	25.9	2.2	14	63.8	3.1	10	78.0	3.2	11
Continental	12.3	1.3	15	14.4	1.2	17	33.6	1.7	16	34.9	1.4	17
Standard (Ohio)	9.7	1.0	16	14.7	1.2	16	29.5	1.5	17	43.4	1.8	15
Skelly	5.0	0.5	17	7.2	0.6	18	12.7	0.6	18	15.8	0.6	18
Phillips	4.5	0.5	18	15.7	1.3	15	51.1	2.5	13	79.9	3.3	10
Ohio Oil Co.	3.6	0.4	19	6.1	0.5	19	9.3	0.5	19	13.3	0.5	19
Total	731.1	79.1		960.6	81.2		1676.4	82.5		1994.9	81.7	
Total U.S.	924.4	100.0		1183.4	100.0		2031.0	100.0		2441.3	100.0	

Source: Company data from Moody's *Industrials*, TNEC *Hearings* (XIV-A), Justice Department Questionnaire, *Annual Reports*, trade journal articles, SEC Form 10-K Reports, and private sources. Totals from Bureau of Mines.

pipe-line domination on the refining stage of the industry must be measured on a local basis (unless the domination be 100 per cent). In order to do this, it is necessary (1) to determine the geographical concentration of all refineries, regardless of ownership, (2) to distinguish between the plants owned by the major oil companies and the independents, and (3) to investigate the

Chart 8

POSITION OF THE MAJOR OIL COMPANIES IN THE REFINING STAGE OF THE INDUSTRY

(Percentage of crude runs to stills)

1930—1952

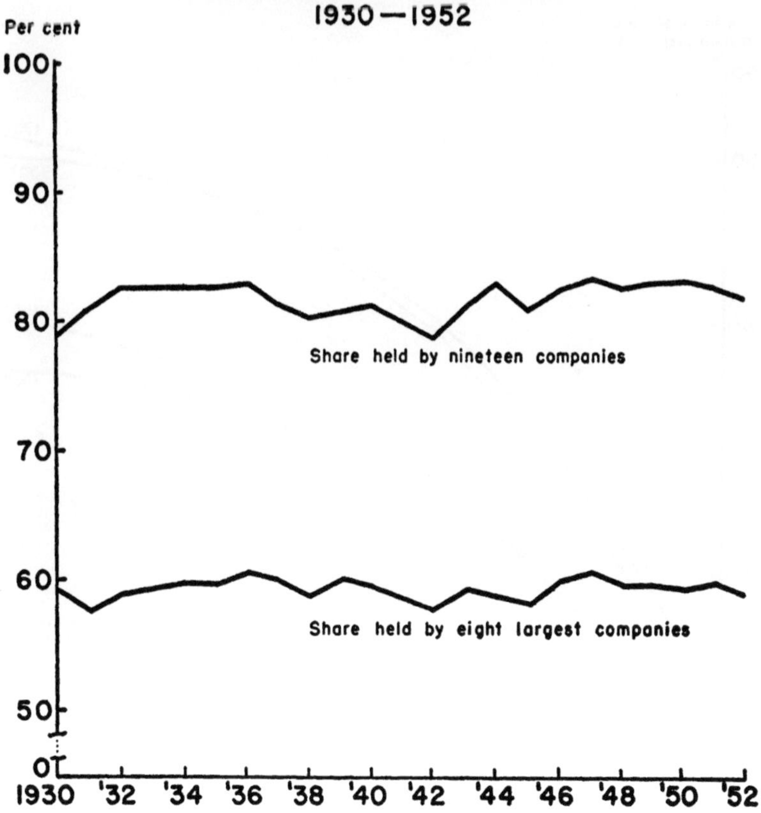

Source: See Table 1.

sizes of any independent refineries which may be found to be properly located as markets for the crude trunk-line system.

(1) *Size and Location of Principal Refining Areas.*—The United States may be divided into some nineteen principal refining areas which account for about 93 per cent of total refining capacity. The remaining areas serve either isolated local markets or relatively small crude fields. The thirteen areas having total

Chart 9

CONCENTRATION IN THE REFINING AND PRODUCING STAGE OF THE OIL INDUSTRY - 1929 AND 1952*

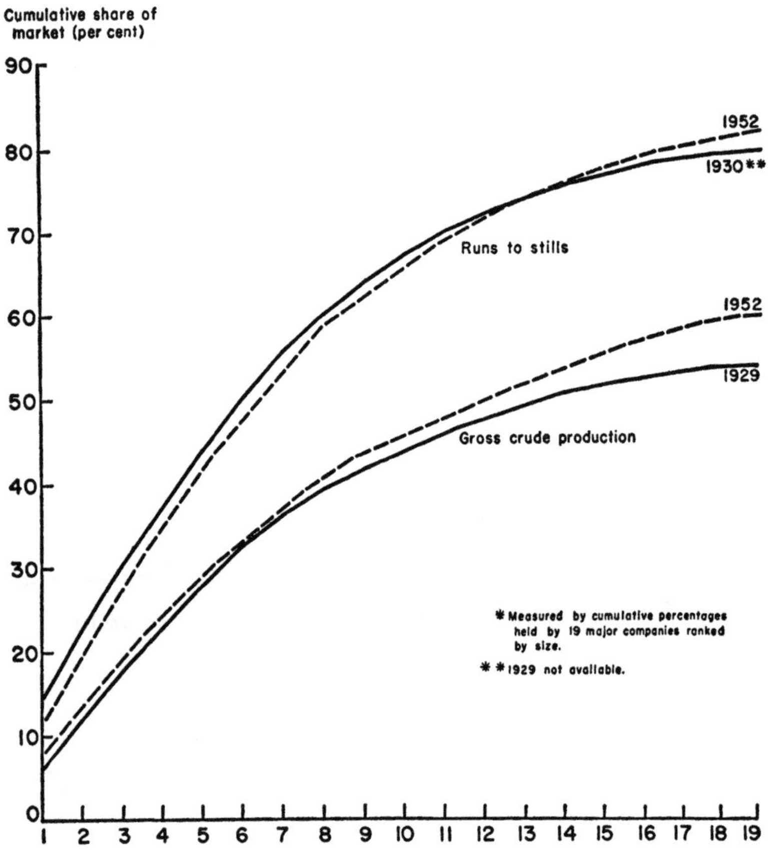

Source: See Tables 4 and 11.

capacities of 100,000 barrels per day or more are shown in Figure 2; the capacities of all areas are shown in Table 4, together with the percentage of total United States capacity accounted for by each. The capacity data represent approximate active capacity as of late 1953. The data are derived from a tabulation by the Petroleum Administration for Defense updated with information in trade journals, especially the *Oil and Gas Journal*.[3]

Figure 2

PRINCIPAL REFINING AREAS OF THE UNITED STATES*

(Late 1953)

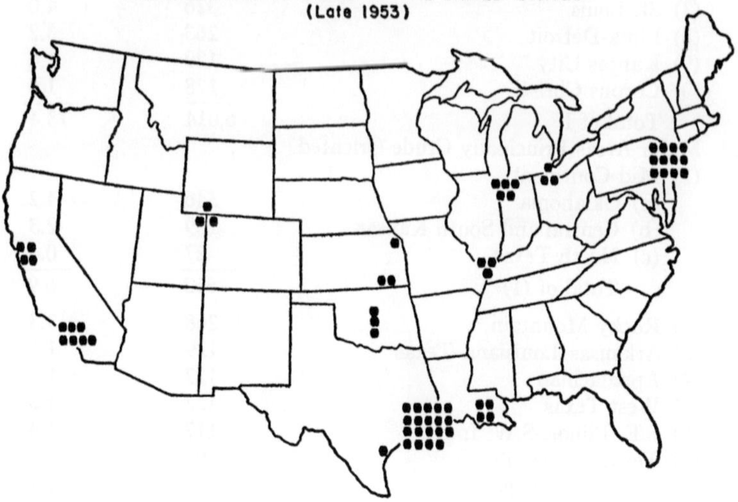

* Accounting for 83% of total capacity

● = 100,000 barrels per day of crude input capacity.

Source: See Table 1.

The principal areas in Part I of the table are:

(1) Houston–Lake Charles — all plants near the Gulf Coast from about fifty miles south of Houston to Lake Charles, Louisiana.

(2) New York–Philadelphia — all plants situated around the ports of New York, Philadelphia, and Baltimore.

(3) Los Angeles Basin — plants in the Los Angeles area.

(4) Chicago — plants located principally on the south shore of Lake Michigan near Chicago.

[3] See issue of March 17, 1952, pp. 321 ff.

TABLE 4

United States Refining Capacity by Areas

Area	Approximate Crude Input Capacity (Barrels per Day)	Per Cent of Total United States
I. Major Areas Not Principally Crude-Oriented		
(1) Houston-Lake Charles	1,920	23.4
(2) Philadelphia-New York	1,204	14.7
(3) Los Angeles	715	8.7
(4) Chicago	535	6.5
(5) Baton Rouge-New Orleans	435	5.3
(6) San Francisco	358	4.4
(7) St. Louis	326	4.0
(8) Lima-Detroit	263	3.2
(9) Kansas City	129	1.6
(10) Corpus Christi	128	1.6
Total of I	6,014	73.4
II. Major Areas Principally Crude-Oriented		
(1) Mid-Continent		
(a) Oklahoma	346	4.2
(b) Central and South Kansas	189	2.3
(c) North Texas	27	0.3
Total of (1)	562	6.9
(2) Rocky Mountain	268	3.3
(3) Arkansas–Louisiana–Texas	129	1.6
(4) Appalachian	122	1.5
(5) West Texas	122	1.5
(6) S.E. Illinois-S.W. Ind.	117	1.4
(7) Texas Panhandle	95	1.2
(8) Central Michigan	93	1.1
(9) Bakersfield	65	0.8
Total of II	1,573	19.2
III. Other		
(1) Cleveland	93	1.1
(2) Louisville	67	0.8
(3) Boston-Providence	55	0.7
(4) Buffalo	42	0.5
(5) St. Paul	33	0.4
(6) Fort Worth	29	0.4
(7) El Paso	27	0.3
(8) Miscellaneous	264	3.2
Total of III	609	7.4
Grand Total	8,196	100.0

[a] Detail does not necessarily add to totals because of rounding.

Sources: Capacity as of 1951 based on PAD tabulation (Petroleum Administration for Defense, *Transportation of Oil*, Washington, 1951, p. 4), and *Oil and Gas Journal* tabulation (March 17, 1952, pp. 321–339) (excludes capacity shut down in early 1951). Approximate additions to capacity from plants reported "building" or "planned" in periodic tabulations (April–August, 1952) of *Petroleum Refiner*, *Petroleum Engineer*, and *Oil and Gas Journal*. Capacities should approximate crude input capacity in late 1953. Percentages computed.

(5) Baton Rouge–New Orleans — principally the great Esso Standard Oil Company refinery at Baton Rouge (the largest in the country at 300,000 barrels per day) and some smaller plants near New Orleans.

(6) San Francisco — all plants in the Bay area.

(7) St. Louis — plants in Southwest Illinois, around Wood River and East St. Louis.

(8) Lima–Detroit — plants located principally in Lima and Toledo, Ohio, and in Detroit.

(9) Kansas City — two refineries located near Kansas City.

(10) Corpus Christi — several relatively small refineries at the port of Corpus Christi, Texas.

The refining areas in Part II of the Table are basically "crude-oriented," while those above are not. In other words, the principal reason for their location is an adjacent supply of crude which may be tapped with small gathering pipe-line systems. In the course of the controversy over crude oil pipe lines, there has been a more or less implicit assumption that all refineries and refining areas constitute markets for crude-oil trunk lines. Upon a moment's reflection, it becomes clear that this assumption is not valid.

Some refineries are located at the source of supply of raw material, that is, in the midst of the oil fields. These are usually small refineries, sometimes medium-sized, which serve local markets. The medium-sized plants often serve more extensive areas than the immediate market by the use of refined products pipe lines connecting them to major markets where other companies may have refineries. However, the majority of refinery capacity is not so located.

Other refineries are located either at "nodal points" or at market centers. "Nodal points" are natural points of transshipment of crude from land to water transportation; often these points are places where crude from more than one field would be brought to the sea in the absence of refineries. Since these refineries are at a point where crude must be shifted from pipe line to tanker, oil may easily be diverted into their stills. Such plants may draw on the field or fields sending crude to the ocean and refine a part of this crude for local use and/or shipment by water in the form of refined products. The alternative available sources of supply tend to relieve the refining center from absolute dependence on one source of crude. Should, for example, the contiguous supply for a crude-oriented plant be exhausted, that plant would face grave difficulties. However, a nodal point refinery on the natural transportation route for crudes from several fields is not solely dependent on one field. Furthermore, if several fields are drawn on, less desirable crudes may be blended with better crudes; this gives the nodal-point refinery advantages over plants located at fields producing only less desirable crudes. An example of a nodal-point area is the Gulf Coast refining area, the largest in the world.

Other refineries may be located at market centers — large or small — for example, those around Chicago, those in Washington state, and other places. The great refining area on the East Coast is there primarily because this is the principal market area in the United States. (These plants also have nodal point advantages in that they can draw on ocean-borne crude from all parts of the world; hence the coastal location as opposed to inland location.)

Of these three general types of location, it is only refineries located at nodal points or at markets distant from crude supplies which can use the services of crude trunk lines. In general it can be said that no refinery is a market for crude trunk lines if it is situated in an area basically because that area contains crude deposits. There are, of course, minor exceptions to any such pronouncement. For example, refineries located in oil fields become potential users of trunk lines once the fields are depleted (if there are other fields not depleted). Similarly, crude producing areas may be overbuilt so that the refining capacity exceeds the local crude producing capacity. But it may be safely said that the areas in the first section of Table 4 represent potential markets for crude trunk lines (either by themselves or for extensions of lines to other areas), while those in the second part do not. In the "other" category there are both refineries at minor crude centers which would not use trunk line crude and refineries at markets where there is not an appreciable amount of capacity. While the latter are trunk line markets, it should be noted that none is large enough for large *economic* crude trunk lines.

It follows that it is only those independent refiners having plants other than crude-oriented plants which can be victimized by major domination of the crude trunk lines. Is this an important group? Table 4 shows that 73 per cent of total refining capacity is situated in the first ten *non*-crude-oriented areas. However, the fact that the majority of capacity owned by all companies is situated where trunk lines are useful does not mean that the majority of the capacity owned by the *small* companies is so situated. Indeed, it is not.

(2) *Location of Major and Independent Refineries.* — In order to determine the location of companies owned by majors and independents, an attempt was made to classify all United States refineries according to the type of location in which they are found. The classification used was: MM, major market; M, substantial market; LM, local market; C, crude-oriented; N, nodal points. All plants classified "C" are implicitly local-market oriented as well (if relatively large, they may serve other markets via products pipe lines). The classification "LM" is reserved for refineries (usually small ones) near urban centers where there is no crude supply in immediately adjacent regions, for example, Seattle, El Paso, and so forth. Those plants classified "MM" are principally market-oriented in very large markets. In some cases more than one code letter was necessary for a plant (or region); for example, a plant in the Houston–Lake Charles region would be classified "N–C–M." This indicates that the probable primary reason for location is the nodal point, but that the refinery also has local crude supplies and a rather substantial local market. Los Angeles plants are classified "MM–C" — major market with a contiguous crude supply, but not a sufficiently large supply for its refining capacity. In the rare cases where the principal reason for the location of a plant was felt to be local crude availability, but where the crude supply is less than the refining capacity by a

considerable amount, for example, Central Michigan, a classification of "C–LM" was used.

The results of this classification are summarized in Table 5, which shows the locational distribution of the capacity of both small and large independents and majors. ("Large" independents

TABLE 5

Distribution of Refinery Capacity in Various Location Classifications among Majors and Independents

Company Groups	Small Independents	Large Independents	Total Independents	Majors	All Companies
N;C;M	3.86	44.04	21.44	32.65	30.30
MM	3.91	10.69	6.88	34.63	28.80
MM;C	10.36	1.00	6.27	9.47	8.79
M	1.55	7.04	3.95	9.41	8.26
N	2.08	—	1.17	—	0.25
C	57.97	24.65	43.40	11.64	18.31
LM	12.73	2.79	8.38	2.13	3.44
C;LM	7.54	9.79	8.53	0.07	1.82
Total	100.00	100.00	100.00	100.00	100.00
Per Cent of Total U.S. Capacity:	11.81	9.19	20.99	79.01	100.00

Notes: MM — major market. M — substantial market. LM — local market. C — crude oriented. N — Nodal (transshipment) point.
Source: See Source of Table 4.

have been defined as those having company capacities of 25,000 barrels or greater.) It will be noted that about 80 per cent of independent refining capacity is located in areas where there are contiguous crude supplies (N–C–M, MM–C, C, C–LM). On the other hand, the plants located in areas which have crude supplies but which are not primarily crude-oriented might wish to utilize crude from outside sources; hence they could constitute a market for the services of crude oil trunk lines. Those independently owned plants in areas not primarily crude-oriented (N–C–M, MM, MM–C, M, N, and LM) account for 48.1 per cent of independent refining capacity, or 10.1 per cent of total United States refining capacity. A tabulation of the plants involved by areas, companies, capacities, and percentage of total refining capacity is shown in Table 6. This table identifies the larger plants in all

TABLE 6

Independent Refineries Which Might Offer Markets for Crude Trunk Lines Because of Type of Location[a]

Company	City	Area (See Table 4)	Type of Location	Capacity (Barrels per Day)	
Large Plants					
Republic	Texas City, Tex.	1	N;C;M	70,000	
Texas City Ref.	Texas City, Tex.	1	N;C;M	60,000	
Eastern States	Houston, Tex.	1	N;C;M	48,000	
Aurora	Detroit, Mich.	8	MM	33,000	
Crown Central	Houston, Tex.	1	N;C;M	32,200	
Southwestern	Corpus Christi, Tex.	10	N;C;M	30,000	
Great Northern	St. Paul, Minn.	—	M	30,000	
Sid Richardson	Texas City, Tex.	1	N;C;M	25,000	
Sunray	Corpus Christi, Tex.	10	N;C;M	25,000	
Taylor	Corpus Christi, Tex.	10	N;C;M	25,000	
Great Lakes Ref.	Blue Island, Ill.	4	MM	20,000	
Pontiac	Corpus Christi, Tex.	10	N;C;M	20,000	
Ashland	Buffalo, N.Y.	—	M	20,000	
Bay Petroleum	Chalmette, La.	5	N;C;M	16,000	
Wood River Ref.	Wood River, Ill.	7	M	15,000	
Ashland	Findlay, Ohio	8	MM	9,500	
Subtotal:				481,700	
Subtotal per cent of Independent Capacity:					28.00
Subtotal per cent of U.S. Capacity:					5.88
Small Plants in Above Areas				220,000	
Calif. Coastal			N	17,400	
Los Angeles			MM;C	108,000	
Subtotal:				345,400	
Grand Total:				827,100	
Grand Total per cent of Independent Capacity:					48.09
Grand Total per cent of U.S. Capacity:					10.09

[a] Those located in regions classified NC–M, MM, MM–C, M, N, and LM.
Source: Tables 4 and 5.

important areas except Los Angeles, which will be discussed in Chapter III (see page 115). These plants may be said to constitute the maximum existing independent refining capacity which could, on the basis of location, suffer from major domination of the crude oil pipe lines. All other existing independents are principally crude-oriented and hence have no use for the services of the major-dominated crude pipe lines.

It should also be noted from Table 5 that capacity owned by the major oil companies in areas which could utilize the services of crude trunk lines amounts to 88 per cent of total major refining capacity. Only 11.64 per cent of the capacity owned by the majors is primarily crude-oriented. The majors have placed their plants principally at the major market or nodal point locations (N–C–M, MM, MM–C, and M together account for 86 per cent of major capacity) and not in the fields.

Hence it is not unnatural to find the major oil companies owning most of the crude trunk lines, while the independents own only small shares therein — the majors need them to the extent of 88 per cent of their refining capacity (70 per cent of total capacity), while existing independents need them only to the extent (as a *maximum*) of 48 per cent of their refining capacity, or 10 per cent of total refining capacity. Furthermore, if we assume that independents located in areas where there are crude supplies can use those supplies to the limit of their needs, then only 20 per cent of independent refining capacity is left at the mercy of the major crude trunk lines. This would mean that only 4 per cent of total existing refining capacity is subject to major control via ownership of the crude trunk lines because of its location (ignoring, of course, the capacity owned by the majors themselves). This figure will be modified even more in Chapter III.

If the independent refiners do not need the major trunk lines, is it possible that they need the majors' refined products lines? This inquiry is not concerned with products lines, but this proposition may be dealt with summarily. In the first place, the independents are more important in refined products pipe-line ownership than in crude-line ownership. In the second place, the *small* crude-oriented refiners in all likelihood serve only local markets (only 25 per cent of the large independents are crude-oriented, while 58 per cent of the small independents are so located). Finally, 88 per cent of the majors' capacity is situated away from the location of the majority of the independent capacity. Under such conditions, the majors' refined products lines would do the independents little good. An independent refiner located in Oklahoma has little use for the services of the majors' refined products line from the Gulf Coast to the Southeastern states. He might well use Great Lakes (from Oklahoma to Chicago) if he were a large independent; but, as will be seen later, the transportation needs of the large independents in the field have been provided for on their own initiative.

(3) *Size of Refineries.* — Are individual refineries large enough to "fit" economic crude pipe lines? If not, then under a program of individual plant ownership of pipe lines there would be bottlenecks of vertical integration. That is, an individual refinery owning its own pipe line could not provide sufficient capacity for an economic line. Under such conditions, lines large enough to realize an appreciable part of pipe-line economies of scale would have to be built either as common carriers or as jointly owned facilities. Even under these conditions the refineries using the lines would have to be closely consolidated geographically in order that the economies of scale of large trunk lines might not be offset by many expensive small lines branching out to individual plants. It is necessary, then, to inquire further into the refinery location problem and to examine the size of plants in the various important refining areas.

The refineries in each of the first ten areas in Table 4 are distributed by capacity ranges in Table 7. These data cover all plants in areas which might use crude trunk lines where the area capacity is 100,000 barrels per day or more. However, it is not necessary to examine Table 7 in order to make a general statement on the relationship of refinery size and pipe-line size. It will be remembered that pipe lines having capacities as high as 400,-

TABLE 7

Distribution of Refineries by Capacity Ranges — Ten Major Areas Not Primarily Crude-Oriented

Capacity Barrels per Day	Areas (1) Houston Lake Charles	(2) New York Phila-delphia	(3) Los Angeles	(4) Chicago	(5) Baton Rouge New Orleans	(6) San Francisco	(7) St. Louis	(8) Detroit Lima	(9) Kansas City	(10) Corpus Christi	Total
	Number of Plants										
0 to 2,500	2		4	2	2			1			11
2,500 to 5,000		1	7			1					9
5,000 to 7,500		2	4	1	2			1			10
7,500 to 10,000			2					1			3
10,000 to 15,000			2								2
15,000 to 20,000		1			1		1				3
20,000 to 25,000		2	1	1				2		1	7
25,000 to 30,000	1							1		3	5
30,000 to 40,000	1			3	1		1	2		1	9
40,000 to 50,000	2					1	1	1			5
50,000 to 60,000	3	1	1								5
60,000 to 80,000	3	2	1		1	2	1	1	2		13
80,000 to 100,000		1		1							2
100,000 to 125,000	2	2	2	1		1					8
125,000 to 150,000	1	1	2								4
150,000 to 175,000	1	1					1				3
175,000 to 200,000	1	2									3
200,000 to 225,000	1			1							2
225,000 to 250,000	1										1
250,000 to 275,000	1										1
275,000 to 300,000											—
300,000 to 325,000					1						1

000 barrels per day were covered in Chapter I, and that transportation costs per barrel-mile were still falling at that capacity level. The largest refinery in the United States (Esso Standard Oil at Baton Rouge) has a rated capacity of 300,000 barrels per day. It is therefore impossible for any one refinery alone to achieve the maximum economies of scale which may be had in pipe-line transportation of crude. On the other hand, it might be possible to achieve fairly low costs with single, "plant facility" crude lines if there were a number of refineries having capacities greater than, say, 200,000 barrels per day — since the cost per barrel-mile falls less sharply after this throughput, even though it falls throughout the range of throughputs. Table 7 shows, however, that there are only five refineries which have crude input capacities of 200,000 barrels per day or more (all giant refineries are in the areas which are not principally crude oriented — see Table 10). The refineries having 200,000-barrel-per-day capacities, or more, account for only 20 per cent of the total capacity in areas which might use crude trunk lines. It is apparent, then, that individual plants alone cannot achieve transportation economies to any great extent.

(4) *Size of Companies (in total and by areas).* — It might be objected that the use of individual plants as the criterion is invalid because one company might own several plants in a given area and could thus realize cheap transportation with its own lines. Table 8 shows the size, area of location (numbered from Table 4), and type of location of the refineries of all companies having total company-wide refinery capacities of 25,000 barrels per day or more. This includes all companies heretofore designated "majors" or "large independents." It will be observed that in only a few instances do the large multi-plant companies have more than one large plant in a given area. Standard (New Jersey) has one plant each in Baltimore and Linden at opposite ends of the New York–Philadelphia region (combined capacity, 240,000 barrels per day); Texaco has two neighboring plants in the Port Arthur area (in area number 1) having a combined capacity of 260,000 barrels per day; Gulf has one plant each in Philadelphia

TABLE 8

Capacity of Refineries Not Principally Crude-Oriented — Companies Having Total Capacities Over 150,000 Barrels Per Day (Late 1953)

Company and Total Number of Plants	N-C-M Plant Capacities	N-C-M Area	MM Plant Capacities	MM Area	MM-C Plant Capacities	MM-C Area	M Plant Capacities	M Area	LM Plant Capacities	LM Area	Total Capacity Not Crude-Oriented	Other Capacity	Total Capacity	Per Cent of U.S.
(1) Standard (N.J.) — 7	300.0	5	185.0	2	—	—	41.5	13	7.5	18				
	260.0	1	55.0	2	—	—	—	—	—	—				
Total	560.0		240.0		—		41.5		7.5		849.0	22.0	871.0	10.6
(2) Standard (Ind.) — 12	130.0	1	208.0	4	—	—	69.0	9	27.0	15				
	30.0	5	6.5	2	—	—	46.0	7	—	—				
Total	160.0		214.5		—		115.0		27.0		516.5	91.0	607.5	7.4
(3) Texas Co. — 14	220.0	1	90.0	4	60.0	3	3.5	13	5.5	17				
	40.0	1	60.0	2	—	—	—	—	—	—				
	—	—	3.5	2	—	—	—	—	—	—				
Total	260.0		153.5		60.0		3.5		5.5		482.5	120.0	602.5	7.4
(4) Socony-Vacuum — 14	175.0	1	104.0	2	125.0	3	30.0	7	12.0	16				
	—	—	31.0	4	4.0	3	22.0	14	—	—				
	—	—	22.5	2	—	—	8.0	13	—	—				
	—	—	22.0	8	—	—	—	—	—	—				
Total	175.0		179.5		129.0		60.0		12.0		555.5	41.0	596.5	7.3
(5) Gulf — 8	245.0	1	183.0	2	—	—	—	—	30.0	18				
	—	—	40.0	8	—	—	—	—	9.5	16				
	—	—	20.0	2	—	—	—	—	—	—				
Total	245.0		243.0		—		—		39.5		527.5	22.0	549.5	6.7
(6) Shell — 5	115.0	1	50.0	6	52.0	3	170.0	7	—	—				
	75.0	5	—	—	—	—	—	—	—	—				
Total	190.0		50.0		52.0		170.0		—		462.0	—	462.0	5.6
(7) Sinclair — 7	115.0	1	105.0	4	—	—	65.0	7	—	—				
	28.0	10	100.0	2	—	—	—	—	—	—				
Total	143.0		205.0		—		65.0		—		413.0	34.0	447.0	5.5

(8) Standard of Calif. — 11	—	—	138.0	6	127.0	—	1.5	13	26.0	15				
	—	—	60.0	2	—	—	—	—	18.0	17				
	—	—	7.2	2	—	—	—	—	6.0	18				
	—	—	—	—	—	—	—	—	6.0	18				
	—	—	—	—	—	—	—	—	1.8	18				
Total	—		205.2		127.0		1.5		57.8		391.5	18.0	409.5	5.0
(9) Phillips — 8	67.0	1	—	—	—	—	60.0	9	5.0	18	132.0	106.3	238.3	2.9
(10) Cities Service — 8	150.0	1	35.0	4	—	—	—	—	—	—				
	—	—	15.0	2	—	—	—	—	—	—				
Total	150.0		50.0		—		—		—		200.0	23.0	223.0	2.7
(11) Atlantic — 2	55.0	1	162.0	2	—	—	—	—	—	—	217.0	—	217.0	2.6
(12) Union — 5	—	—	82.8	6	111.0	3	—	—	4.0	18	197.8	11.6	209.4	2.6
(13) Tide Water — 4	—	—	85.0	6	14.0	3	—	—	—	—				
	—	—	80.0	2	—	—	—	—	—	—				
Total	—		165.0		14.0		—		—		179.0	27.0	206.0	2.5
(14) Sun — 2	—	—	140.0	2	—	—	—	—	—	—				
	—	—	65.0	8	—	—	—	—	—	—				
Total	—		205.0		—		—		—		205.0	—	205.0	2.5
(15) Standard (Ohio) — 4	—	—	36.5	8	—	—	92.5	11	16.5	12				
	—	—	21.0	8	—	—	—	—	—	—				
Total	—		57.5		—		92.5		16.5		166.5	—	166.5	2.0
Grand Total	2005.0		2213.0		493.0		609.0		174.8		5494.8	515.9	6010.7	73.3
Total U.S.	2483.1		2360.7		715.1		744.0		319.7		6622.6	1573.2	8195.8	100.0

Notes: Areas —
(1) Houston — Lake Charles
(2) Philadelphia — New York
(3) Los Angeles
(4) Chicago
(5) Baton Rouge — New Orleans
(6) San Francisco
(7) St. Louis
(8) Lima — Detroit
(9) Kansas City
(10) Corpus Christi
(11) Cleveland
(12) Louisville
(13) Boston — Providence
(14) Buffalo
(15) Salt Lake
(16) Fort Worth
(17) El Paso
(18) Miscellaneous

Source: See Source of Table 4.

and on Staten Island (combined capacity 203,000 barrels per day); Socony has two plants in the New York area (combined capacity, 126,500 barrels per day). No other important cases exist. When the capacities greater than 200,000 barrels per day are added to the refineries having 200,000 barrels per day of capacity, only 29 per cent of total refining capacity in areas which might use crude trunk lines is accounted for (200,000 barrels of the Texaco capacity at Port Arthur were already included).

Consequently, it may be stated that no single company has sufficient capacity in any given refining area to get the cheapest transportation which can be had with available sizes of pipe, even if all its crude came through the same pipe line. However, some companies could get fairly cheap transportation on their own for plants having 29 per cent of the relevant capacity. As a result, if maximum economies are to be achieved it is necessary to utilize joint transportation of oil to the principal areas. How many areas, if any, are large enough to permit even highly efficient *joint* transportation by all companies having plants therein?

(5) *Refining Area Size.* — The size of the relevant refining areas is shown in Table 4, Part I. (The other areas are irrelevant, since they are either crude-oriented or have less than 100,000 barrels per day of refining capacity.) All but two of these areas could, if we were to re-design the pipe-line system, support at least one crude pipe line large enough to take advantage of a considerable degree of pipe-line economies of scale. Five of these areas have combined capacities greater than 400,000 barrels per day, while two others have capacities greater than 325,000 barrels per day. However, these areas are in some cases rather extensive and in some cases have contiguous crude supplies. For example, the Houston–Lake Charles area covers a good many miles and is in the heart of the prolific Gulf Coast field. Nevertheless, it is still large enough for several major interregional lines (which it currently has); one line, indeed, serves plants at both ends of the area and in the middle (the terminal is in the middle, with branches to either end). The Detroit–Lima, Kansas City, and

Corpus Christi areas are too small in themselves for lines carrying very large throughputs. On the other hand, the first two of these areas can be served (as they are) with extensions of large lines to other areas. Corpus Christi is served principally by local crude, with some West Texas crude via a small line.

In sum, no single plant and no single company can achieve maximum pipe-line transportation economies on its own. These could be achieved, however, in the principal refining regions which need crude trunk lines. The extent to which they *have* been achieved will be a matter for subsequent discussion.

(6) *Plant and Company Capacities of Majors and Independents.* — Not only can no company achieve the most economical transportation with only its own oil, it would also be impossible for all independent refiners located in areas other than crude-oriented regions to achieve economic transportation without the use of the majors' oil. This may be seen by referring to Table 6, which shows the independent refining capacity which might use crude trunk lines. The total of this capacity for the country as a whole is only about 800,000 barrels per day, and this capacity is scattered all over the western half of the country. A joint-venture line between the Gulf Coast and Illinois independents would hardly be an economic success. If they drew all their crude from the same source, the independent refiners in the Houston–Galveston area could muster 235,000 barrels per day of capacity and could thus support a reasonably economic line. None of the others could, and these companies would without doubt (as they do) utilize crudes from several sources. It follows, then, that not only is it natural to expect the majors to own the lion's share of trunk lines, it is also necessary for independents to use the same lines used by the majors if they (the independents) are to achieve economic transportation. Without economic transportation, the market-oriented independent refiners can hardly be expected to be an important competitive force in the industry — if they could exist at all.

How important a competitive force are the independents? This subject will be discussed in detail later, but it is appropriate to note the size of individual independent companies and plants here. One or two general statements can be made upon the basis of Table 8. The largest "independent" (Ashland) has a company capacity of 124,500 barrels per day, compared with the national total of some 8196 thousand barrels per day. This, the largest of the independents (a firm which is in reality integrated), accounts for only 1.5 per cent of total United States refining capacity. The largest individual plant owned by an independent has a capacity of 70,000 barrels per day; this places it thirtieth in size among refineries. Half of the nation's refining capacity is accounted for by plants having capacities of 80,000 barrels per day or more (see Table 9). The largest independent refinery, then, is smaller than twenty-nine plants which together make up over half of all refining capacity.

The sizes and the locations of major and independent refineries are shown in detail in Tables 9 and 10. Table 9 shows the size of all plants of small and large independents, the majors, and all companies combined. Note that total independent refining capacity is 21 per cent of all refining capacity. Table 10 shows the size of the plants of independents and majors by location classification. Note that only three of the independent refineries having capacities of 25,000 barrels per day or more are crude-oriented. This means that, in general, those independents who locate away from the crude supplies have the largest refineries. If there are economies of scale associated with crude refining, then the few independents located at markets are at least those best able to compete with the majors.

In short, Tables 8, 9, and 10 show clearly that even though the independents together account for some 20 per cent of refining capacity, the existing independents in terms of individual company capacity or individual plants are not very significant in relation to total refining capacity.

(7) *Summary.*—The discussion of the structure of the refining stage of the industry may now be summarized: (a) Independents account for about 20 per cent of United States refining

TABLE 9

Percentage of Refinery Capacity in Various Capacity Ranges — Majors and Independents

Capacity Range (Barrels per Day)	Small Independents	Large Independents	All Independents	Majors	All Companies
	Cumulative Percentage of Capacity				
0 to 2,500	100.0	100.0	100.0	100.0	100.0
2,500 to 5,000	90.9	99.7	94.8	99.9	98.8
5,000 to 7,500	74.8	98.8	85.3	99.3	96.4
7,500 to 10,000	54.4	96.6	72.9	97.9	92.7
10,000 to 15,000	45.5	94.3	66.9	96.9	90.6
15,000 to 20,000	24.7	87.1	52.0	96.1	86.9
20,000 to 25,000	17.8	83.0	46.3	93.6	83.6
25,000 to 30,000	—	80.3	35.1	91.0	79.2
30,000 to 40,000	—	67.0	29.3	88.0	75.7
40,000 to 50,000	—	45.3	19.8	84.0	70.6
50,000 to 60,000	—	38.9	17.0	79.4	66.3
60,000 to 80,000	—	17.3	7.6	73.7	59.8
80,000 to 100,000	—	—	—	63.6	50.3
100,000 to 125,000	—	—	—	57.0	45.0
125,000 to 150,000	—	—	—	45.0	35.6
150,000 to 175,000	—	—	—	34.9	27.6
175,000 to 200,000	—	—	—	27.4	21.7
200,000 to 225,000	—	—	—	19.0	15.0
225,000 to 250,000	—	—	—	12.4	9.8
250,000 to 275,000	—	—	—	8.7	6.8
275,000 to 300,000	—	—	—	4.6	3.7
300,000 to 325,000	—	—	—	4.6	3.7
Total Capacity (000 barrels per day):	968	753	1,721	6,475	8,196

Source: See Source of Table 4.

capacity (1721 thousand barrels per day, out of a total capacity of some 8196 thousand barrels per day). (b) Most of the independent capacity is crude-oriented and hence has little use for the service of crude trunk lines. (c) The preponderance of major capacity is not crude-oriented. (d) The few independent plants which do compete with the majors in locations away from the

TABLE 10

Number and Size of Refineries in Various Types of Areas — Majors and Independents

Capacity Range (Barrels per Day)	N–C–M In-dep.	N–C–M Ma-jor	— MM — In-sep.	— MM — Ma-jor	MM–C In-dep.	MM–C Ma-jor	— M — In-dep.	— M — Ma-jor	— N — In-dep.	— N — Ma-jor	— C — In-dep.	— C — Ma-jor	— LM — In-dep.	— LM — Ma-jor	C–LM In-dep.	C–LM Ma-jor	All Areas In-dep.	All Areas Ma-jor	All Com-panies
0 to 2,500	4	—	3	—	3	—	—	1	2	—	43	2	15	2	3	—	73	5	78
2,500 to 5,000	—	—	1	1	6	1	1	1	5	—	24	6	8	—	2	1	47	10	57
5,000 to 7,500	2	—	2	2	4	—	—	—	—	—	21	8	6	5	3	—	38	15	53
7,500 to 10,000	—	—	1	—	3	—	—	1	—	—	7	5	1	1	1	—	13	7	20
10,000 to 15,000	—	—	—	—	1	1	—	—	—	—	14	2	5	3	3	—	24	6	30
15,000 to 20,000	1	—	—	1	—	—	1	—	—	—	3	6	—	2	1	—	6	9	15
20,000 to 25,000	1	—	1	4	1	—	1	1	—	—	5	4	—	—	—	—	8	9	17
25,000 to 30,000	3	1	—	1	—	—	—	—	—	—	1	5	—	—	—	—	5	7	12
30,000 to 40,000	2	1	2	3	—	—	1	1	—	—	—	1	—	1	—	—	4	7	11
40,000 to 50,000	1	1	—	1	—	—	—	2	—	—	—	3	—	—	—	—	1	7	8
50,000 to 60,000	—	—	—	2	—	1	—	—	—	—	2	1	—	—	—	—	2	4	6
60,000 to 80,000	2	5	—	3	—	1	—	3	—	—	1	1	—	—	—	—	3	13	16
80,000 to 100,000	—	—	—	4	—	—	—	1	—	—	—	—	—	—	—	—	—	5	5
100,000 to 125,000	—	2	—	3	—	2	—	—	—	—	—	—	—	—	—	—	—	7	7
125,000 to 150,000	—	2	—	2	—	2	—	—	—	—	—	—	—	—	—	—	—	6	6
150,000 to 175,000	—	—	—	1	—	—	—	1	—	—	—	—	—	—	—	—	—	2	2
175,000 to 200,000	—	1	—	2	—	—	—	—	—	—	—	—	—	—	—	—	—	3	3
200,000 to 225,000	—	1	—	1	—	—	—	—	—	—	—	—	—	—	—	—	—	2	2
225,000 to 250,000	—	1	—	—	—	—	—	—	—	—	—	—	—	—	—	—	—	1	1
250,000 to 275,000	—	1	—	—	—	—	—	—	—	—	—	—	—	—	—	—	—	1	1
275,000 to 300,000	—	—	—	—	—	—	—	—	—	—	—	—	—	—	—	—	—	—	—
300,000 to 325,000	—	1	—	—	—	—	—	—	—	—	—	—	—	—	—	—	—	1	1
Total Plants	16	17	10	31	18	8	4	12	7	0	121	44	35	14	13	1	224	127	351

Source: See Source of Table 4.

field are for the most part the largest independent refineries; but even the largest independent refinery ranks only about thirtieth among all plants.

C. CRUDE PRODUCTION

It is now necessary to investigate the relative positions of majors and independents in the crude producing stage of the industry. In addition, we must examine the size of the various producing areas in order to establish the amounts of crude available for trunk lines — if there were no large fields, there could be no large trunk lines.

An ideal approach to an investigation of the size of the supply of crude for trunk lines would follow in general that used for refineries. Unfortunately, data on individual company holdings in the various fields or in broad areas are not available. However, it is the producing capacity of *regions* which is important for the purposes of this study. There is no need of location classifications, since all crude production is (naturally enough) crude-oriented, be it major or independent production.

In evaluating the competitive ability of market-oriented independent refineries, it might be of some interest to know their distance from independent crude supplies compared with the distance of major refineries from their own crude supplies. Aside from this, there is no real need of company capacity data by areas. Even this is probably not too important, since it is safe to assume that there is some independent producing capacity in all large producing areas. Consequently, this study will rely on intercompany comparisons on a nation-wide basis when comparing major and independent companies. The size of producing areas need not be distributed among the various companies.

(1) *Size of Principal Producing Areas.* — Data on crude oil "availability" (production capacity) were assembled and published by the PAD in 1951 in order to determine the amount of pipe-line capacity needed out of each of the principal producing

areas.[4] These figures on "MER" [5] productive capacity by major regions as tabulated from the PAD study are shown in Table 11.

An examination of the data in Table 11 reveals that nine regions have an anticipated MER in 1953 greater than 300,000

TABLE 11

MER for Various Producing Areas as Predicted by the PAD in 1951

Area	1951	1952	1953	1954	1955
	00's of Barrels Per Day				
(1) Appalachian	50.5	47.5	44.5	41.5	39.5
(2) Ill., Ind., Ky., Mich., Ohio, Tenn., & Mo.	266.4	261.6	255.8	249.0	242.2
(3) Kansas	306.0	310.0	313.0	315.0	317.0
(4) Okla.	517.0	540.0	565.0	580.0	600.0
(5) Miss., Ala., & Fla.	111.5	114.5	117.5	120.5	125.5
(6) Ark. & N. La.	206.0	207.0	208.0	208.0	207.0
(7) La. Gulf Coast	550.0	610.0	650.0	675.0	700.0
(8) Gulf & S. Texas	1171.0	1217.0	1254.0	1280.0	1297.0
(9) East Texas	514.0	525.0	531.0	537.0	540.0
(10) No. Tex., Central Tex., & W. Central Tex.	293.0	310.0	325.0	336.0	343.0
(11) Texas Panhandle	90.0	89.0	88.0	87.0	86.0
(12) W. Tex. & N. Mex.	1395.0	1492.0	1567.0	1616.0	1650.0
(13) Rocky Mountains	327.2	346.0	364.5	376.4	386.0
(14) California	986.0	991.0	995.0	995.0	990.0
Total	6783.6	7060.6	7278.3	7416.4	7523.2

Source: Petroleum Administration for Defense, *Transportation of Oil* (Washington, 1951), Exhibit 6 following p. 8.

barrels per day. However, in computing the amount of oil available for crude pipe lines local crude-oriented refining capacity and water transportation of oil cannot be ignored. Table 12 indicates the amount of crude available for shipment from each of the important areas once local refinery capacities have been subtracted from the MER in 1953. In addition, allowance has been made for normal inland water-borne traffic as computed by the

[4] See PAD, *Transportation of Oil,* Exhibit 6, following p. 8.

[5] MER production is the "maximum efficient rate" of production from a field such that ultimate recovery will be maximized.

TABLE 12

Net Export Crude Production Capacity, by Region (1953 Estimate)

Area	MER	Local Refinery Capacity	Net for "Export"
	000 Barrels Per Day		
(1) Gulf Coast & S. Tex.	1827	2048[a]	−221
(2) Phila.-N. York	0	1204	−1204
(3) Los Angeles	350	715	−365
(4) Chicago	0	535	−535
(5) Baton Rouge-N. Orleans	0	435	−435
(6) San Francisco	0	358	−358
(7) St. Louis	0	326	−326
(8) Lima-Toledo-Detroit	0	263	−263
(9) Kansas City	0	129	−129
(10) Corpus Christi[b]	—	—	—
(11) Oklahoma	540	346	194
(12) Kansas	310	201[c]	109[d]
(13) Rocky Mountain	346[d]	266[d]	80[d]
(14) W. Tex.-N. Mex.	1567[d]	124[d]	1443
(15) Ark.-La.-Tex.	539	129	410
(16) S.E. Ill., S.W. Ind.	188	117	71
(17) Appalachian	50	122	−70
(18) Central Mich.	37	93	−56
(19) N. Texas	325	27	298
(20) E. Ky.	28	53	−25
(21) Miss., Ala., Fla.	107	9	98
(22) San Joaquin	543	65	478
Total Available for "Export"			3181

[a] Houston-Lake Charles plus Corpus Christi.
[b] Included in (1).
[c] Includes 12,000 barrels per day included in miscellaneous in Table 1 (Western Kansas).
[d] Western N. Mex. (2450 barrels per day refining, less than 1000 prod.) included in number (14).
Source: MER from Table 12. Refining Capacity from Table 4.

PAD.[6] (This procedure is similar to that used by the PAD in Exhibit 8, following page 42.) It is apparent from Table 12 that there are in reality only a few "net-producing" regions (those which produce more than the local refining capacity) which have oil available for "export" to the rest of the United States. Of these the most important are West Texas, Ark-La-Tex,

[6] See PAD, *Transportation of Oil*, pp. 46 ff.

the San Joaquin Valley, Oklahoma, and the Rocky Mountain states. Indeed, one can almost say that the total crude capacity of the net-producing regions (minus their local refining capacity) is the available supply of crude oil for major interregional trunk pipe lines. This figure of some 3181 thousand barrels per day is less than one-half of the average daily output as of mid-1953.[7]

There are, however, limitations involved in using these MER capacity data (adjusted for crude-oriented refineries) as anything more than rough measures of the amount of crude oil available for pipe-line shipment. In the first place, the companies owning the pipe lines from a given area may well not be the same companies which own refineries in this area. If the pipe-line owners want to try to purchase all the oil in the field for their own use, then they would build sufficient pipe-line capacity for the field capacity less *their* capacity in the area, not less *total* refining capacity in the area. Why should a company having no refinery in the area automatically concede crude to the local refineries? Consequently, in a peacetime, competing market, it may not be valid to subtract all crude-oriented refining capacity from the field capacity. On the other hand, the MER is *not,* under conditions short of total war, the expected production rate in the principal producing state. In Texas, it is true that fields theoretically produce at the MER rate per *day;* but under the allowable system they are only permitted so many per month, say 20, at this rate. Twenty producing days would mean that something less than one-third of the MER productive capacity is actually shut in.[8] While it is desirable in periods of total war to have pipe-line capacity sufficient to meet the MER plus a safety factor (minus local refining needs and water transport, if any), it is on the surface somewhat unlikely that private companies would consider the usable crude supply in, say, West Texas, to be as great as the MER in peacetime periods.

[7] See Bureau of Mines, *Monthly Petroleum Statement,* July 1953, p. 2.

[8] It was indicated in the Railroad Commission allowable hearings of February 18, 1953 that "daily" MER figures provided by the companies are probably a bit higher than a true daily MER — say 1+ day's MER. Hence the fact that 20 days at MER means a little more than 20/30 production.

These two limitations may be illustrated by the West Texas case. The completion of pipe lines under construction or planned from West Texas to the North and to the Gulf and Pacific Coasts would give a total crude capacity out of West Texas of some 1890 thousand barrels per day,[9] compared with an MER of 1618 thousand barrels per day (as estimated by the PAD) and local refinery capacity of 217 thousand barrels per day (West Texas plus Texas Panhandle from Table 4). This may mean that the company groups which have recently completed large lines out of West Texas either estimate the MER at a higher level than that predicted by the PAD, or intend to compete with the local refineries for the crude.

The problem of actual production rates less than MER is in general only important in Texas (see Table 13). It is only under great economic pressure that the other states cut production to help keep crude prices stable. Table 13 shows, using the PAD prediction of MER as an approximate production capacity, that Texas is the only state which normally shuts in any appreciable percentage of its production. This is best illustrated in the summer of 1953 (see August 1953 in Table 13), when, after a period of inventory accumulations, Texas cut production repeatedly while the other states stood idly by. It was only in 1954 that other states made any production cuts of significance, and these only followed still greater cuts in Texas. It might be said that Texas, having the most to lose from crude price declines since it is the largest producer, acts as the "umbrella" at all times to keep the price of crude stable — just as United States Steel is supposed to have done in past depressions for the steel industry. (The Texas Railroad Commission complains that the other states do not "play the game" fairly.)[10]

The final limitation involved in using the PAD MER predictions to measure the sizes of sources of supply is that they *are* predictions. That predictions of future crude availability are

[9] See *World Oil,* October 1953, pp. 154–155; this figure includes the proposed line to the West Coast which had not been started as of late 1954.

[10] Allowable hearings, November 14, 1953.

TABLE 13

Estimated MER Versus Actual Production in Major Producing Areas

	1951			1952			August 1953		
	PAD MER 000 Barrels Per Day	Actual Production 000 Barrels Per Day	Actual as Per Cent of MER %	PAD MER 000 Barrels Per Day	Actual Production 000 Barrels Per Day	Actual as Per Cent of MER %	PAD MER 000 Barrels Per Day	Actual Production 000 Barrels Per Day	Actual as Per Cent of MER %
Appalachian	51	50	98	48	49	102	45	47	104
Mid-West	266	274	103	262	276	105	256	269	105
Kansas	306	314	103	310	314	101	313	328	105
Oklahoma	517	512	99	540	526	97	565	580	103
Miss., Ala., Fla.	112	106	95	115	103	90	118	103	87
La. and Ark.	756	718	95	817	742	91	858	791	92
Texas-New Mexico	3463	2912	84	3634	2966	82	3765	3053	81
Rocky Mountain	327	300	92	346	304	88	365	414	113
California	986	971	99	991	982	99	995	999	100
	6784	6157	91	7063	6262	89	7280	6584	90

Source: MER See Table 11. Actual production from Bureau of Mines, *Monthly Petroleum Statement*.

TABLE 14

Gross Crude Production of Nineteen Major Oil Companies, 1929, 1937, 1948, and 1952

	1929			1937			1948			1952		
	Production (000,000 Barrels)	% of U.S. Total	Rank	Production (000,000 Barrels)	% of U.S. Total	Rank	Production (000,000 Barrels)	% of U.S. Total	Rank	Production (000,000 Barrels)	% of U.S. Total	Rank
Shell	58.0	5.8	1	54.8	4.3	5	102.2*	5.1	4	127.0	5.5	3
Socony-Vacuum	57.8	5.7	2	61.7	4.8	2	76.8	3.8	8	91.3	4.0	7
Gulf	57.5	5.7	3	55.9	4.4	4	100.2	5.0	5	95.2	4.2	6
Standard (N.J.)	51.7	5.1	4	80.9	6.3	1	180.6	8.9	1	171.7	7.5	1
Standard (Calif.)	51.5	5.1	5	48.2	3.8	7	105.0	5.2	3	105.8	4.6	5
Texas Co.	50.4	5.0	6	60.5	4.7	3	113.6	5.6	2	131.0	5.7	2
Continental	36.1	3.6	7	48.5	3.8	6	89.1	4.4	7	83.6	3.6	8
Ohio Oil Co.	32.3	3.2	8	27.3	2.1	13	38.8	1.9	13	37.4	1.6	16
Tide Water	24.7*	2.5	9	28.0	2.2	11	42.5*	2.1	10	45.5	2.0	12
Cities Service	22.3	2.2	10	28.0	2.2	11	36.5	1.8	14	42.6	1.9	14
Union	20.6	2.0	11	21.2	1.7	15	36.3	1.8	15	40.8	1.8	15
Pure	18.4*	1.8	12	22.3	1.7	14	32.2	1.6	17	30.4	1.3	17
Sinclair	18.3	1.8	13	34.8	2.7	9	41.6	2.1	11	49.1	2.1	10
Phillips	14.4	1.4	14	29.1	2.3	10	68.7*	3.4	9	72.8	3.2	9
Skelly	9.8	1.0	15	12.8	1.0	18	26.0*	1.3	18	27.9	1.2	18
Sun	7.6	0.8	16	14.6	1.1	17	41.2*	2.0	12	46.2	2.0	11
Standard (Ind.)	7.3	0.7	17	39.8	3.1	8	93.8*	4.6	6	123.7	5.4	4
Atlantic	5.9	0.6	18	15.5	1.2	16	36.2*	1.8	16	44.8	2.0	13
Standard (Ohio)	—	—	19	—	—	19	13.1*	0.6	19	14.3	0.6	19
Total	544.6	54.1		683.9	53.5		1274.4	63.1		1381.1	60.3	
Others	462.7	45.9		595.3	46.5		745.8	36.9		910.9	39.7	
Total U.S.	1007.3	100.0		1279.2	100.0		2020.2	100.0		2292.0	100.0	

* Estimated.
Source: Company data from Moody's *Industrials*, TNEC *Hearings* (XIV-A), Justice Department Questionnaire, *Annual Reports*, trade journal articles, SEC Form 10-K Reports, and private sources. Totals from Bureau of Mines.

subject to some considerable error is obvious. However, the point should be raised. As the PAD cogently puts it, "unforeseen new producing areas will be found . . . Lack of knowledge as to the future automatically and unavoidably introduces an area of underestimation of transportation requirements."[11] It is also possible, if not likely, that some areas might be smaller than foreseen. The predictions used in Table 11 are, however, probably as good as can be had. They were made by an agency staffed by industry personnel who are certainly no less qualified to predict than anyone else. The PAD data on MER can be accepted with as little reservation as is possible when predicting future crude reserves and availability. Indeed, the close relationship between production and predicted capacity (shown in Table 13) is a compliment to the accuracy of the PAD's predictions.

(2) *Size of Companies in Crude Production.* — While company data are not available by areas, company crude production (not capacity) figures are available for the country as a whole. Table 14 indicates the approximate share of "gross" crude production held by each of the majors for the years 1929, 1937, 1948, and 1952. The total accounted for by these companies in relation to total United States production is shown in Chart 10 for the period 1929 through 1952, as well as in Chart 9 above for 1929 and 1952. The percentage of gross crude production held by the majors is considerably less than their share of refining. The majors' share of crude production has also been less stable than their share of refining, since there was a distinct increase during World War II; some of this increase has since been mitigated.

Chart 10 also shows the majors' share of "net " crude production. "Net" crude production is total production by a company less royalties and partnership holdings, while "gross" production includes royalties (and sometimes partnership interests). The proper measure of market control would be net production plus royalties, since the royalty owners have no effective control over "their" share of the oil; indeed, they are paid in cash, not in oil. However, some companies, for example, Continental, report

[11] PAD, *Transportation of Oil,* p. 8.

Chart 10

POSITION OF THE MAJOR OIL COMPANIES IN THE CRUDE PRODUCTION STAGE OF THE INDUSTRY

(Percentage of U.S. crude production)

1929 — 1952

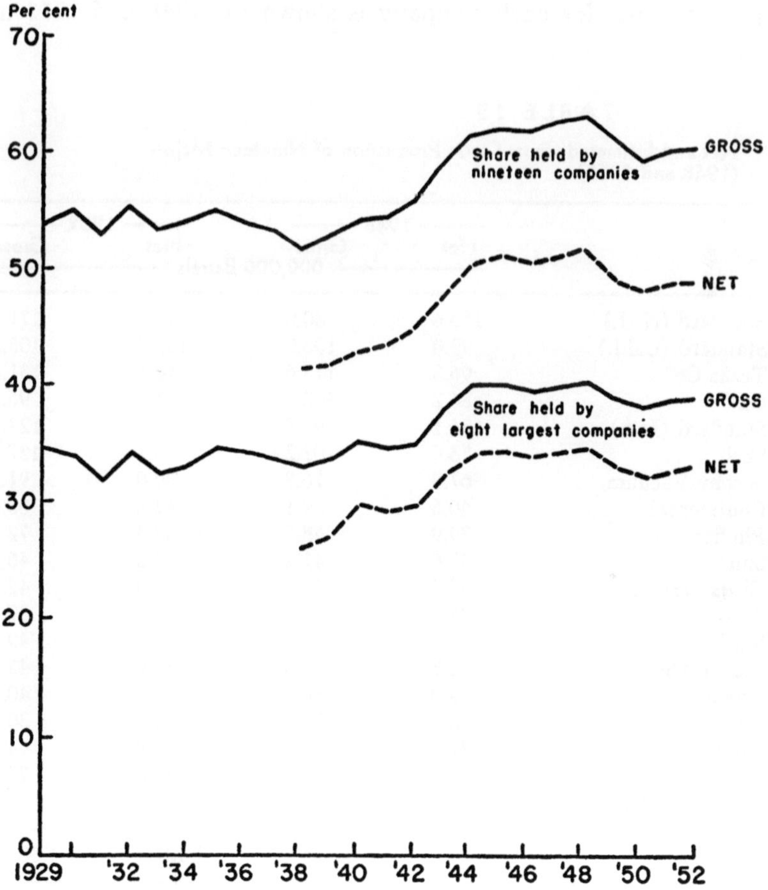

Source: See Table 14.

partnership holdings in gross production, thereby overstating their share of the market (and hence overstating the majors' share). Consequently, gross production overstates the majors' share, while net understates. The proper figure should be somewhere between the two, but much closer to gross. The proper spread between gross and net is shown in the lines on Chart 10 for the eight largest companies, which do not include partnership holdings in their gross data. Their gross production is probably their share of the market. The extent of the difference between gross and net for each company is shown for 1948 and 1952 in Table 15.

TABLE 15

Net and Estimated Gross Crude Production of Nineteen Majors (1948 and 1952)

	1948		1952	
	Net	Gross	Net	Gross
	000,000 Barrels			
Standard (N. J.)	156.6	180.6	148.6	171.7
Standard (Calif.)	99.0	105.0	102.3	105.8
Texas Co.	96.3	113.6	110.5	131.0
Gulf	86.2	100.2	81.8	95.2
Standard (Ind.)	84.1	93.8	97.3	123.7
Shell	78.6	102.2	96.1	127.0
Socony-Vacuum	67.9	76.8	80.0	91.3
Continental	40.6	89.1	42.8	83.6
Phillips	39.9	68.7	42.3	72.8
Sun	37.6	41.2	42.2	46.2
Cities Service	37.0	36.5	38.9	42.6
Ohio Oil Co.	35.2	38.8	33.9	37.4
Sinclair	33.7	41.6	45.5	49.1
Tide Water	32.7	42.5	35.0	45.5
Union	29.9	36.3	33.7	40.8
Pure	28.1	32.2	26.5	30.4
Atlantic	27.3	36.2	33.8	44.8
Skelly	22.2	26.0	23.8	27.9
Standard (Ohio)	11.4	13.1	12.4	14.3
Total	1,044.3	1,274.4	1,127.4	1,381.1

Source: Company data from Moody's *Industrials*, TNEC *Hearings* (XIV-A), Justice Department Questionnaire, *Annual Reports*, trade journal articles, SEC Form 10-K Reports, and private sources. Totals from Bureau of Mines.

The share of production capacity held by independent producers in 1953 may be estimated from Table 14. The independent producers' output in 1952 was 910.9 million barrels (2489 thousand barrels per day) based on major gross production of 1,381.1 million barrels (3784 thousand barrels per day). Since the latter is slightly overstated, independent production might be estimated at 2500 to 2550 thousand barrels per day, or some 800,000 barrels per day more than independent refining capacity as of the end of 1953. It is necessary to compare independent production with independent refining *capacity* because production capacity data are not available by companies. However, this affects only Texas independents to any extent in the 1953 figures, since other states produced more or less at capacity (see Table 13). Total independent production capacity, then, was somewhat more than 2500 thousand barrels per day in 1953; but the normal effective capacity in the light of the Texas Railroad Commission's allowable policies can be approximated by this figure.

III

THE CONTROVERSY OVER CRUDE OIL PIPE LINES

Two general remedies have been proposed for the problems which are said to have arisen from ownership of the pipe lines by the large companies:[1] (1) outright divorcement of crude pipe lines from the major companies by antitrust action, the lines subsequently to be operated as true common carriers with service available to all refiners and producers, large and small alike, and (2) forcing the major companies to operate their own lines as true common carriers at low rates. While successful vertical disintegration of the oil industry from the application of the antitrust laws has not taken place since 1911 (when the old Standard Oil Company was broken up), something approaching the second regulatory system has been used since 1941.

The "Consent Decree" in the Atlantic Refining case (a Sherman Act proceeding instituted by the Department of Justice) limits dividends from the operation of crude oil pipe lines to 7 per cent of the investment; earnings over this may be used for working capital and expansion of facilities (the new facilities not to be counted in the rate base).[2] The Interstate Commerce Commission also regulates rates under the authority granted it by the Hepburn Act of 1906.[3] The ICC holds earnings in excess of 8 per cent to be unreasonable.[4] The effect of this dual regulation by the Justice Department and the ICC is that rates on inter-

[1] See G. S. Wolbert, *American Pipe Lines* (Norman, Okla., 1952), p. 33, fn. 1, for reference to some of the bills and hearings.

[2] See *U.S.* v. *Atlantic Refining Co.*, Civil No. 14060 D.D.C., December 23, 1941. The decree is reprinted in Wolbert, *Pipe Lines*, pp. 165–169.

[3] "The provisions of this Act shall apply to any corporation or any person or persons engaged in the transportation of oil . . . by means of pipe lines . . . who shall be considered and held to be common carriers." XXXIV Statutes 584 (1906), Fifty-ninth Congress.

[4] See Wolbert, *Pipe Lines*, p. 21.

state shipments of crude oil in pipe lines are limited to levels which yield about 8 per cent on the investment, with dividends limited to 7 per cent. Not only are rates regulated, common-carrier status is enforced by the ICC to a greater or lesser extent. The principal purpose of this is to attempt to assure "ratable" (proportional) taking of oil from all companies, be they majors or independents.

This makeshift regulation of pipe lines as common carriers has not, however, satisfied those who would dis-integrate the oil industry; and it does not even seem to satisfy some who advocate common-carrier regulation at low rates. In any event the controversy over crude oil pipe lines did not by any means end in 1941. It might be of some value to discuss the entire history of the controversy in some detail; however, in this monograph the discussion may be limited principally to the proposals put forward in recent years by two of the more sophisticated examiners of the problem, Professor Eugene V. Rostow and Professor George S. Wolbert, Jr. An examination of their views will provide a sufficient exposition of both sides of the controversy.[5] Other recent enlightened discussions of the pipe-line problem can be found in the works of Professor Bain and Professors McLean and Haigh.[6] Before evaluating the positions of Professors Rostow and Wolbert, it is in order to summarize their points of view briefly, at least as this writer interprets them. This is done in Section A of this chapter. The majority of the chapter (Section B) is devoted to an evaluation of the positions of Rostow and Wolbert.

A. THE CONTROVERSY SUMMARIZED

Rostow's Original Position. Professor Rostow's views were first expressed in his monograph entitled, *A National Policy for the*

[5] In Wolbert, *Pipe Lines,* section 2, the history of the controversy is discussed in some detail.

[6] See (1) J. S. Bain, *Economics of the Pacific Coast Petroleum Industry* (Berkeley, Calif., 1944–1947), especially chapter vi, part ii, and pp. 45–48 and 86–91, part iii; and (2) J. G. McLean and R. W. Haigh, *The Growth of the Integrated Oil Companies* (Boston, 1954), especially chapter vii.

Oil Industry; they were later expanded and developed to some extent in an article in the *Yale Law Journal.*[7] In short, Rostow's position is that ownership, and thus control, of pipe lines is the "chief weapon" used by the major oil companies in stifling the existing independent refiner, in stifling new entry into the refining business (and perhaps into crude production, although this point receives relatively little attention), and in protecting their (the majors') position in the market for crude oil. Not only does ownership of the pipe lines by the majors stifle the independence of existing and potential non-integrated refiners, it also keeps the independent out of the market-oriented locations and remits him "largely to shifting and unsatisfactory locations in the field."[8] Rostow concedes, of course, that pipe lines have functions other than market control; but he is convinced that they are more than a "productive piece of equipment." They are also "a necessary element for the preservation of the special conditions of market structure in the petroleum industry on which price leadership and price maintenance ultimately rest."[9] The mechanism of this market control is a denial of access to the lines (either direct denial or by charging rates which are high enough to discourage independent shipments).

Rostow's solution to the problem posed in these terms is vertical dis-integration of the industry into four segments: producing, refining, transportation, and marketing,[10] together with horizontal dis-integration of the very large companies in each stage of the industry.[11] A further integral part of his program would involve compulsory unitization of the oil fields and an end to crude oil price control through state regulatory agencies.

In *A National Policy for the Oil Industry* there is little comment on the details of such a program of reorganization of the

[7] See E. V. Rostow, *A National Policy for the Oil Industry* (New Haven, 1948), and E. V. Rostow and A. S. Sachs, "Entry Into the Oil Refining Business: Vertical Integration Re-examined," 61 *Yale Law Journal* 856–914, June–July 1952.

[8] Rostow, *National Policy,* p. 58.

[9] *National Policy,* p. 66.

[10] *National Policy,* p. 145.

[11] *National Policy,* p. 118.

transportation (or other) stages of the industry. Likewise, there is little effort to answer the common arguments presented against independently owned pipe lines. Some rebuttal is made of pro-major arguments based on the existence of economies of scale in the operation of refineries and large companies as a whole, but there is little if any attention to pipe-line economies of scale. Rostow is content to propose a public policy of vertical and horizontal dis-integration by antitrust dissolution procedures which he assumes would produce the goals he desires: an industry with no vertical integration (except that arising from the growth of existing independent companies)[12] and with many companies in each stage, each so small as to be unable appreciably to influence price.[13] Rostow rejects rate regulation as a complete, or even a very important partial, solution of the pipe-line problem.[14] He concedes that if equal access to the lines were achieved by rate regulation, there would be a "qualified" solution to the problem (this is the point of divorcing them from the majors). While Rostow is not among those who have contended that there can never be competitive equality if an independent pays a major for the use of the latter's line,[15] he is convinced that rate regulation alone cannot achieve a complete solution. Why? In the first place, existing lines were not built to make money as common carriers, but to carry the builders' oil [16] (and also, according to Rostow, to enforce market control). The integrated oil company will prefer its own shipment to that of the independent when the lines are full (as they should be for efficient operation), regardless of rates. (Rostow might have added that the incentive for the major to carry the independent's oil would hardly be increased by government action to reduce the rates he can charge.) Second, he believes that any rates that would be approved by the ICC would be

[12] Rostow, *National Policy*, pp. 123–124.

[13] Rostow and Sachs, "Entry," p. 861.

[14] Rostow, *National Policy*, pp. 62–63.

[15] *National Policy*, p. 65. An example of this position is found in the TNEC *Hearings*, Part 15, p. 8167. The question of paying a competitor for the use of his facilities is discussed in M. A. Adelman, "Integration and Antitrust Policy," 61 *Harvard Law Review* 1289 (1948).

[16] *National Policy*, p. 62.

high enough to act as a competitive deterrent to the independent. Furthermore, even if the independent crude seller did get access to the distant refinery markets, the larger number of buyers which he would find there would be more than offset by the larger numbers of his fellow independent producers who could reach the common refinery areas.[17] It should be pointed out that this second reason for rejecting rate regulation implies that independent producers have some local monopoly powers in bargaining with the majors at the field—powers which would be lost, to the independents' disadvantage, if refiners could choose from many independent producers at refining centers.

Wolbert's Position. Professor Wolbert cites four reasons for major domination of the pipe-line stage of the industry:[18]

(1) *The "tremendous initial outlay of capital" required for long lines.* This eleminates from consideration small firms which cannot afford to build the long lines.

(2) *The great "hazard or risk" that the original investment can never be amortized.* If the field dries up before the line is paid out, the builder does not get all of the initial investment back. "These risks necessitate pipe line ownership by large corporations whose assets can survive these occasional mishaps."

(3) *The interdependence of pipe line and refinery.* Oil companies believe that constant flow to the refinery can best (only?) be achieved by a "plant facility" pipe line connecting refinery with field. Whether or not vertical integration is in reality an economic necessity, the large oil companies *think* it is; and this is what matters. The large companies believe that refineries should have their own pipe lines. Since most of the nation's refining capacity is owned by the large companies, it follows naturally that most of the pipe-line capacity is also owned by the large companies, if for no other reason than that pipe lines are built for refineries.

(4) *Defensive integration.* If one large company is dependent on another for its transportation facilities and is paying rates higher than "cost," it will be inclined to build its own line. Since

[17] *National Policy,* p. 63.
[18] Wolbert, *Pipe Lines,* pp. 10–12.

only large, integrated oil companies can be expected to build large lines (following the logic of the first three points), these companies naturally come to own the preponderance of pipe-line capacity.

None of these points mentions market control. Unlike Rostow, Wolbert does not believe that the pipe lines were built by the majors as instruments of market control. He feels that pipe-line ownership by the majors is attributable to these four factors which represent normal business reactions to financial, technical, and competitive conditions, rather than an attempt to dominate the market for crude oil.

Wolbert does, however, concede that the pipe lines once charged the highest rate the traffic would bear and thereby imposed a real competitive disadvantage on the independents.[19] Not only were rates high, Wolbert also believes that minimum tenders have been too high in the past. Some minimum is necessary (Wolbert prefers 5000 barrels), but tenders as high as 100,000 barrels have been used to keep the independents out of the lines.[20] On the other hand, Wolbert does not believe that crude pipe lines refuse to act as true common carriers today. (This is not true of *products* pipe lines, most of which have been built as plant facilities.) He concedes the truth of our quotation from Mr. Shatford[21] — but that was in 1904. Discrimination among crude suppliers is now prohibited by state statutes.[22] Ratable (proportional) taking is now the practice (even at capacity), he contends, except for very minute shipments. He finds the contrary claims in the TNEC *Hearings* unimpressive, and cites an interesting example of ratable taking in 1947 (a period of almost full-capacity crude production). A major company had a crude supply agreement with an independent producer which changed its mind and sold to an independent refiner; the major then carried the oil for the independent refiner in its own line.[23] Fur-

[19] *Pipe Lines*, pp. 20–21.
[20] *Pipe Lines*, p. 25.
[21] See page 4 above.
[22] Wolbert, *Pipe Lines*, pp. 42–43.
[23] *Pipe Lines*, p. 47, fn. 261.

thermore, shipments of outside oil for the account of independents are believed to be on the upswing in recent years.

Nevertheless, Wolbert admits that the volume of outside shipments is much lower than in other common-carrier forms of transportation. There are also good reasons for this. In the first place, "The great majority of independent refiners are located in the producing areas and have their own gathering or short pipe lines. Thus they are at the wrong end of the line." [24] In addition, there are several lesser reasons. From the point of view of the independent refiner, there is a time lag if he buys oil in the field and waits until *that* oil is delivered to him. Furthermore, he must invest in the complete pipe-line fill while his oil is being shipped. Minimum tender requirements must be met if the independent would stand to lose by contamination of his crude by lower-grade crude. Bookkeeping problems arise upon buying in the field.[25] In sum, it is simpler, and perhaps cheaper, for the independent refiner to buy from the pipe-line company, even in the case of market-oriented independent refiners who have their own crude holdings. These companies, he says, prefer to sell to majors in the field and buy from major pipe lines at the site of their refineries.[26] Only in periods of a strain on crude supply is the independent refiner likely to get out and beat the bushes for his crude. As far as the independent producer is concerned, his "bargaining position would be no better, and possibly not so good, if he sought to sell the crude at the refinery gates." (This is strangely like Professor Rostow's curious argument noted above.) [27] Furthermore, the independent producer's capital is tied up while he seeks a buyer. Again, it is simpler to take the line of least resistance and sell to the major with the pipe line.

Wolbert's opinions differ from Rostow's in another important respect: he believes that dis-integration of the oil industry is an inappropriate solution to the pipe-line problem. To some extent this is doubtless attributable to the fact that he does not, as has

[24] *Pipe Lines,* p. 45.
[25] *Pipe Lines,* p. 46.
[26] *Pipe Lines,* p. 46.
[27] See page 80 above.

been pointed out, believe that part of the pipe-line problem exists any longer. This is the matter of conscious exclusion of the independents from the pipe lines. On the other hand, he points out that appreciable government regulatory effort (to be discussed below) was necessary to force rates down to their present level: "the record of the major companies in the absence of any regulation is not calculated to reassure the worried independent operator." [28] Furthermore, and most important, it is Wolbert's belief that the independent operates at a competitive disadvantage, even if admitted to the lines, if there is a difference between the rates charged and the major's cost of operating the pipe lines (where "cost" includes some allowance for a normal return on the investment).[29] For these reasons, Wolbert does not reject public policy completely. He does, however, reject divorcement of pipe lines as an acceptable policy for a number of reasons. Since these reasons are representative of the usual defense of integrated lines, they must be examined in some detail.

In the matter of pipe lines, Wolbert believes that independent pipe lines resulting from a program of dis-integration would face serious economic difficulties. This argument is based in part on the historic fate of two independent crude pipe lines (erroneously referred to as the only two) which were dismal failures. One of these lines, the Prairie Pipe Line Company, was a company divorced from the original Standard Oil Company; as such it should provide an acceptable example of what might happen to divorced pipe lines. This line prospered at first, "due to the large volume of business tendered by its former owner, the major purchaser in the Mid-continent field." [30] However, this crude purchaser was forced to withdraw from the Mid-Continent field as a purchaser after loss of its former (refinery) outlets. Prairie Pipe Line withered away and died. The other example is the Crusader Pipe Line project which was constructed as a new line to carry oil as a common carrier from the Arkansas fields to the

[28] Wolbert, *Pipe Lines,* p. 22.
[29] *Pipe Lines,* pp. 20 and 52.
[30] *Pipe Lines,* p. 102.

Mississippi River (apparently seeking barge purchasers for an outlet, since there is no refinery at this location). This pipe line "never carried a barrel of oil," as he puts it.

In addition to the historical examples of failures of independent pipe lines, Wolbert has other reasons for his misgivings about the feasibility of new independent pipe lines. The most important objection is that a company engaged solely in transportation will be considerably less eager either to extend existing systems or to build new lines to new producing areas than would an integrated company seeking to improve its reserve position.[31] Building crude oil pipe lines to new areas is risky because the ultimate capacity of a new field cannot be precisely predicted. Suppose a field which had at first appeared to be large proved to be small? The integrated company is willing to take the chance to improve its reserve position. The non-integrated pipe line would have no such incentive and would hesitate to make the large investments required.

Furthermore, if independent pipe lines were not so interested in building capacity to new areas as integrated companies are, then wildcatting by non-integrated operators (as all operators would perforce be under a program of dis-integration) would decrease. The reason for this is that pipe-line connections are necessary if oil is to be salable in markets away from the fields; without a market, there is no incentive to drill. Lessened wildcat activity would, in turn, make the independent pipe lines even more reluctant to build new lines to new fields. The non-integrated producers would want an assurance of transportation facilities before drilling and the non-integrated pipe lines would want an assurance of drilling before laying. (This problem is like that faced by the Western railroads after the Civil War — without them there could be no great population in the West, but without the population there could be no successful railroads.)

Insofar as independent refiners are concerned, Wolbert distinguishes between those existing now and those which might appear in the future. Existing refiners would, he feels, not be

[31] *Pipe Lines,* p. 103.

particularly affected by dis-integration because divorcement would not change the location of the existing pipe lines.[32] For this reason no help would be given to the crude-oriented refiners who account for the bulk of independent capacity. Furthermore, those independents who could use the lines because of favorable location would be competing for the services of the non-integrated lines with the refineries of the former owners of the pipe lines. When the lines are at capacity, it would be only reasonable to expect the independent pipe-line company to give preference to the large buyer (its former owner) in order to assure itself of as constant a market as possible. Furthermore, Wolbert contends that any new pipe lines that might possibly be built by non-integrated pipe-line companies would be built to areas where there are large refineries, not to areas where there are small independent refiners. Finally, a "pipe line entrepreneur whose sole interest is making a profit from pipe lines is apt to seek higher rates than the refinery-owner whose primary object is to obtain a continuous supply of crude or a steady outlet for his refined products." [33]

These comments apply to existing independent refiners. In the case of new independent refiners that might appear in the future, Wolbert is also not impressed with the value of vertical dis-integration of the oil industry. He concedes that the most "persuasive argument in favor of divorcement" is that it would create more competition (from independents) in the refinery market by giving independent refiners access to crude.[34] Even so, he does not consider the chance of increased capacity to be very great:

> It is contrary to common experience to believe that the mere divorcement of pipe lines would counteract the effect of large buying power. The independent producer would rather sell his oil to a steady, large volume buyer than to a fly-by-night who might give a premium today but shift his purchase the next day and never buy the producer's oil again. The independent pipe line owners would be just as inclined to favor their large customers, the major refiners, as would present pipe line management . . . Even assuming *arguendo* that divorcement of

[32] *Pipe Lines,* p. 100.
[33] *Pipe Lines,* p. 100.
[34] *Pipe Lines,* p. 103.

pipe lines would cause independent refiners to spring up in the populated market centers, the effect would only be to foreclose the present independent refiners in the field, with the majors acquiring some of the field location business in the process.[35]

This quotation contains the extent of Wolbert's rebuttal to "the most persuasive" reason for dis-integration.

Wolbert, then, believes that independent pipe lines would fare badly after divorcement, that existing independent refiners would not be helped to any extent, and that there would be no real incentive to create new independent refinery capacity. He also comments on the effect of dis-integration on independent producers. As was pointed out above, independent producers do not, according to Wolbert, have much incentive to use the pipe lines now because they prefer to sell in the field. For this reason they would also probably not be particularly affected by divorcement, except in the case of marginal or submarginal firms. These producers would probably be adversely affected, since majors now subsidize marginal or submarginal fields where they have existing pipe-line connections.[36] In the event of divorcement, the majors would have no further reason to buy from the relatively high-cost producers.

The discussion of Wolbert's views may be concluded with a brief statement of his positive views on public policy toward pipe lines. He would, first, eliminate the consent decree and return control of the lines to the ICC. Then he would enlarge that agency's staff devoted to pipe-line regulation, with the aim of achieving "cost" rates for all pipe lines.[37] These rates would cover operating expenses and a minimal return on the investment. Wolbert believes that once "cost" rates were achieved, the principal disadvantage suffered by independent refiners would disappear, since the independent refiner would get his transportation at "cost," the best he could hope for even if he had his own pipe lines. (Like Rostow, Wolbert recognizes for the most part that

[35] *Pipe Lines,* pp. 103–104.
[36] *Pipe Lines,* p. 101.
[37] *Pipe Lines,* pp. 160, 163, and 21.

if the independent pays "cost" it makes no difference whether he pays it to a major or to someone else.) Similarly, the companies owning the lines would get their transportation at "cost." Competition among large and small refiners would then be based on costs of refining per se, with no advantage accruing to the major from ownership of his own pipe line. Since Wolbert believes that the problem of physical access is unimportant, he makes no particular provisions for solving it except to continue the present ICC regulations which require ratable taking. With "cost" rates and ready access to the pipe lines, those few independent refiners who can use crude pipe lines will have no valid complaint.

Rostow's Reply. In the recent *Yale Law Journal* article, Rostow's views have not changed appreciably. "The vertical integration of the large companies, despite some pipe line rate reductions, still seems to function as the key factor permitting them to influence the price of crude, to limit the amount of independently refined crude reaching consuming markets, and thus to maintain a semblance of order in the pricing of final products." [38]

The major part of the article by Rostow and Sachs, excluding that dealing with general antitrust matters, is devoted to rebuttal of Wolbert's arguments. It is necessary to summarize their positions on each of Wolbert's major points.

(1) *The Efficacy of Rate Regulation.* Conceding that the test period for the 7 per cent ceiling on dividends under the consent decree has been short and has been punctuated by periods of construction material shortages, Rostow believes that the decree has done little to help the existing independent refiners change gasoline prices or marketing practices.[39] Neither has it helped promote entry into refining. If a dozen years of rate regulation have failed to do these things, why expect future rate regulation to accomplish them? It is true that rates have fallen to some extent, but Rostow and Sachs contend that such progress as has been made by independent refiners since 1941 has come from those who

[38] Rostow and Sachs, "Entry," pp. 898–899.
[39] "Entry," p. 902.

have freed themselves in one way or another from reliance on the majors for crude. Independent refiners have not, according to Rostow and Sachs, progressed because of lower pipe-line rates.

Furthermore, Rostow and Sachs assert that "cost" rates mean rates which cover operating costs and include a long-run "normative" return on capital, and that such returns "by no means correspond to the rates" which are normally accepted as constituting a fair return on investment.[40] The authors apparently believe that a program of cost rates as Wolbert uses the term would be less than the fair-value rate that commissions would award. Hence the program is unacceptable.

Finally, Rostow and Sachs object that "rate regulation is incapable, as a matter of practical experience, of achieving so precise a result as rates which would at any moment of time yield 'cost rates' " — or any other precise return.[41] The process of public utility regulation can not be sufficiently accurate to guarantee any given rate, in this instance one neither higher nor lower than "cost."

In short, Rostow feels that rate regulation has not helped solve the pipe-line problem historically, that "cost" rates would be too low for the Constitutional requirements for rate making, and that public utility regulation is not capable of being sufficiently precise to assure that cost rates would ever be cost rates. This being the case, he rejects Wolbert's proposed public policy and maintains his original belief in dis-integration. He also disputes Wolbert's views about the dangers and futility of dis-integration.

(2) *Importance of Access of Independent Refiners to Crude.* Rostow and Sachs consider the various arguments advanced by Wolbert to show that independents do not care whether they have access to crude in the field to be "hardly substantial." [42] Loss of capital (for a time) while the oil is in transit, delay while waiting for one's own oil, bookkeeping problems, common stream

[40] "Entry," p. 885.
[41] "Entry," p. 885.
[42] "Entry," p. 895.

versus segregated shipments, all these are negligible problems which cannot be so important as Wolbert believes. Furthermore, there is no reason why new pipe lines should favor existing refineries. Should they locate their terminals near existing refineries, as would be expected, there is no reason why independent refineries cannot be built in the same area where they can be connected by inexpensive short lines to the main lines.

(3) *Effect of Divorcement on Marginal Producers.* The independent producer who might be harmed by divorcement of pipe lines because he is a marginal or submarginal operator is rejected by Rostow and Sachs. If these companies are inefficient, then it is hardly a defense of integration "in the name of the competitive system" that the major oil companies continue under integration to buy dear oil, when they could get cheap oil elsewhere, "because they have made a mistaken investment to a field which turns out badly." [43]

(4) *Effect of Divorcement on Existing Pipe Lines.* Rostow and Sachs do not share Wolbert's fears of the effect of divorcement on existing pipe lines. They point out that there are other historical examples of independent lines than those cited by Wolbert, and that these lines still operate today, over forty years after they were divorced from the old Standard Oil Company.[44] Furthermore, they contend that the respective fates of independent pipe lines competing with major pipe lines and independent pipe lines competing in an industry where there are *only* independent pipe lines are two different fates indeed.[45] It is, they say, really not valid to attempt to surmise the economic success of pipe lines which might be divorced from what has happened to pipe lines in the past, when there was no general program of dis-integration and when the independent pipe line had to compete with integrated lines.

Furthermore, they contend with apparent validity that independent pipe lines would have the same incentive to leave their

[43] "Entry," p. 897.
[44] "Entry," p. 884, fn. 98.
[45] "Entry," p. 897.

lines in marginal fields as would integrated companies "so long as any return above actual operating costs is earned on the carriage, or while operating losses are less than shut-down losses," that is, while price is greater than average variable cost.[46] Whether the pipe line is integrated or non-integrated is irrelevant. This follows the accepted economic doctrine that a firm should operate as long as the costs incurred by operating (that is, all the costs which are not fixed costs incurred at zero output) are less than the revenue which would accrue from operation. (Under these conditions, the firm would be better off, even though operating at a net loss, than if it had remained shut down.)

(5) *Effect of Divorcement on New Pipe Lines.* In reply to the all-important assertion that non-integrated pipe lines would be reluctant to build to new fields, Rostow and Sachs first state that the majors "may" throw lines into new areas which have not been proved. This is not, however, an unmixed blessing: "From the point of view of society, if not of the individual leaseholder in the field, it would surely be preferable to delay the investment in pipe until the field's prospective yield is more firmly established."[47] The apparent conclusion is that independent pipe lines would be less eager to build new lines immediately and, indeed, that this is to be preferred.

On the other hand, Rostow and Sachs make a positive contention that it is difficult to see why independent pipe lines would be more reluctant to build to new areas as "some students of the industry" have suggested. The reason for this is that the independent lines, even though they have no concern as purchasers of crude, "would have strong interests in gaining first access to a new field for the prospective transportation business."[48] As evidence they cite the eagerness of independent natural gas pipe lines to build lines, even though they own next to no reserves of their own.[49]

In sum, the position of Rostow and Sachs on this question is

[46] "Entry," p. 897.
[47] "Entry," p. 896.
[48] "Entry," p. 896.
[49] "Entry," p. 896.

not clear. On the one hand, they contend that it would be better to have non-integrated pipe lines since the majors build too fast; this perforce means that they think that majors build faster than would independents. On the other hand, they contend that independents would build just as fast as majors.

(6) *Effect of Divorcement on New Refining Capacity.* Rostow and Sachs take Wolbert to task for his brief reference to the problem of entry into refining (see page 85 above). Their position on this matter is clear: they believe that entry into refining is free, given equal access to crude oil supplies.[50] This access could be provided by divorcement of the pipe lines and their subsequent operation as common carriers taking all oil offered, on a ratable basis if necessary. Since this is one of Rostow's chief reasons for insisting on dis-integration, it is necessary to examine such evidence as he has assembled supporting the contention of free entry.

In actuality little factual evidence is presented. There are no real answers to such questions as:

> Is the price of crude relatively so high, and the price of gasoline so low, as to make independent refining an unattractive field for investment? Is the cost of efficient refining so high that capital requirements alone constitute an insuperable barrier to independent expansion? Is the refining business more risky than other parts of the industry, at least in the sense that the rewards can never be quite so spectacular as in oil production, whereas the pressure in years of severe price difficulty can be very real? What significance, if any, should be attached to pipe line ownership by the major companies as a factor limiting the growth of existing independent refineries, and the entry of potential independent companies in this part of the business?[51]

These questions are posed but not answered. Rostow and Sachs simply assert that these problems and the problem of the formidable buying power of the majors "could not decisively affect the competitive position of new entrants into the refining business" if there were equal access to the pipe line. Rostow and Sachs are

[50] "Entry," pp. 898–899.
[51] "Entry," p. 881.

"inclined to disagree with Wolbert" and to believe that entry into refining is relatively free.

One question was investigated to some extent; this is the problem of the minimum efficient size of refineries. Are there important economies of scale in the operation of refineries? The authors found that those companies having total refining capacities, not plant capacities, less than 50,000 barrels per day in 1946 grew at a less rapid rate between 1940 and 1951 than did the larger companies. Indeed, the share of refining held by the majors was found to be the "highest" in the history of the industry (since 1911 of course).[52] However, the alleged decline of the independents can, they assert, "hardly be attributed to technological imperatives based on economies of scale." Why? Because they find that small refineries are not less efficient than large ones and that technical economies depend on plant, not company, size. The evidence is the following:

> Several independent refiners have stated in their replies to questionnaires that in their experience the minimum efficient scale of refining is currently between 5,000 and 12,000 barrels per day capacity. One such response, based on engineering estimates, is that a well-located Mid-Continent refinery using catalytic cracking, could be altogether efficient at a capacity of 15,000 barrels per day, and would cost approximately $15,000,000. Another places the minimum efficient size of a competitive refinery in his district at 17,500 barrels per day capacity. Dr. Robert E. Wilson, Chairman of the Board of Standard Oil Company (Indiana), has recently said that a diversified products refinery of 30,000 barrels per day capacity is large enough to be reasonably efficient, although "maximum efficiency and minimum costs would require throughputs several times this," with the result that several refineries have been built up to handle over 200,000 barrels per day — a small fraction of the total current national capacity of about 7,000,000 barrels a day.[53]

This paragraph reporting a speech and the results of questionnaires to independents contains all of the cost evidence presented.

[52] It was, by the way, 0.9 percentage points lower in 1952 than in 1932, an insignificant difference. (See chart 8.)

[53] Rostow and Sachs, "Entry," p. 890. Text refers to R. E. Wilson, "Is Big Business Bad? — Fact vs. Fiction 3" (reprint of speech before Anti-Trust Symposium of Chicago and Illinois Bar Associations, Chicago, January 8, 1952).

It is unfortunate that the authors were not able to provide complete cost curves. As will be discussed in the succeeding evaluation of the controversy, others have obtained cost data.

B. THE CONTROVERSY EVALUATED

With this discussion of the "controversy" in mind, it is now possible to review and evaluate the points raised. Emphasis will be laid on the probable effect of the two public policies proposed (divorcement and cost rates) on pipe lines and refining, since these are the keys to the problem. Independent producers have a total output of some 2500 barrels per day, compared with independent refining capacity of 1720 thousand barrels per day. For the independent producer to be helped by any public policy toward pipe lines, that policy must promote the creation of new independent refining capacity to remove this disparity. It is true that if the pipe lines were, for example, divorced and made into non-integrated common carriers, then independent producers would gain access to refineries located at market areas. But to what avail if they found only the existing refineries there? Since the majors dominate refineries located at market centers, the independent producers would have substituted the opportunity to sell to the large majors at the refinery for the opportunity to sell to the same large majors in the field; this would hardly be an improvement. The only way to create new alternative markets for the independent producers is to create new efficient independent refining capacity.

As far as independent marketers are concerned, both Wolbert and Rostow link their fate to that of the independent refiner. Only if new independent refining capacity should arise, would there be opportunities for new alternative sources of supply to the independent marketers. Some objection might be raised to the proposition that independent jobbers are in reality dependent on independent refineries, since there are many non-integrated marketers who use major refinery products. (Two such large independents are Standard (Kentucky) in the Southeast and Jenney in New England.) This is, however, not particularly relevant when predicting the effect of divorcement on independent jobbers. Those now using major refined products would be unaffected, unless the majors' transportation costs rose; in this case the independent jobber might well be worse off under a policy of divorcement, since refined product prices might rise at the refinery. In any event, the independent marketers at the major market areas would be no better off if no new independent refining capacity were created, since the independent marketers are dependent on refineries located at market centers for their products.

In short, the crux of the matter is the effect of the proposed policies on refineries and pipe lines — both existing and new refineries and pipe lines. The points which deal specifically with independent producers will be discussed first. Then the more important matters may be considered.

(1) *The Position of Independent Producers.* Two assertions have been made by Rostow and Wolbert concerning the effect of divorcement and compulsory cost rates on independent producers. One of these concerns the majority of such production; the other concerns marginal independents.

Rostow and Wolbert apparently agree that the independent producers have some local-monopoly bargaining power when selling to the majors at the field. Were they to attempt to sell their oil at refining centers they would only find more intensified competition, since all their brethren would also be attempting to sell there. Furthermore, the independent is selling to majors at the refining centers just as he would at the field. What has he achieved? At the cost of tying up his capital while the oil is in transit, he is selling to the same people. There might theoretically be more majors in a refining center than in any given field, but it must be remembered that it is the large majors which are the important purchasers. These companies are active in nearly all principal producing areas, and, indeed, would be expected to have their own transportation facilities to most producing areas. All of the eight largest majors, for example, have their own pipe-line service out of the West Texas area (see Table 2).

Furthermore, the price of crude is stabilized by state proration. Consequently, even if new refining capacity were created, there would probably be no change in crude oil pricing — short of the end of proration. (The end of the allowable system is, of course, a part of Rostow's policy.) Finally, it might well take a *very* large increase in well-located independent refining capacity to change the structure of the crude market appreciably, even apart from prorationing. Other industries have stable prices without state regulatory assistance. Competitive pricing of crude would be likely only if a large number of new alternative purchasers appeared.

In the matter of *marginal* producers, as opposed to the bulk of the independents, there is some disagreement between Wolbert and Rostow. Wolbert thinks that non-integrated pipe lines would not take "dear" oil because they have no refineries in which to use it. In order for a marginal (to be precise, a *sub*marginal) producer to be able to sell his oil in competition with other oil at a refining center, he would have to have a rate concession from the independent pipe-line company. Rostow and Sachs reply that it is no defense of integration that integrated companies might operate inefficient capacity while non-integrated companies would not. More to the point, they say that as long as out-of-pocket expenditures by the pipe line are less than what it can get for carrying the marginal oil, any pipe line — integrated or independent — would have an incentive to transport the oil.

This is true *only* if there is excess capacity in the line when all available efficiently produced oil has been taken in. Under such conditions an independent marginal producer might be able to strike a bargain with the independent pipe line to carry his inefficiently produced oil at a rate less than the average total cost of transportation but greater than average variable cost, so that he could afford to sell it in competition with cheaper crude at the refining centers. Whether the pipe line or producer would absorb the greater part of the loss would be a matter of relative bargaining power. The most important determinant of bargaining power would be the relative amounts of efficient and inefficient production in the area served by the line — the higher the amount of efficient production, the less the bargaining power of the producer.

It must be pointed out that there is a legal objection to this relatively sound economic argument. Unless all oil carried in the line came from the same inefficient field, rate *discrimination* would be necessary on the part of the pipe line in favor of marginal producers. One doubts that the proponents of dis-integration would approve of a public policy which permitted discriminatory rates, since the independent pipe lines would be tempted to discriminate in favor of their large customers (the majors), thereby removing the equal transportation opportunities which dis-integration was designed to establish. On the other hand, an integrated company could use the marginal oil without discrimination by buying it at the field and shipping on its own account at a "loss" in the pipe line, provided always that the net increment in revenue from the whole operation (transporting, refining, and marketing) was greater than the incremental cost involved. Alternatively, an integrated line might set its rate structure so that the marginal oil could be carried; this would give it a pipe-line "loss" on its own oil, but this "loss" would be recouped in the rest of the integrated process.

Finally, this problem is probably not very important in any event, since the amount of very high-cost production, such as that in fields using secondary recovery, is quite small in relation to total output. The more important problem is the effect of divorcement on efficient producers. Both Rostow and Wolbert seem to think this effect to be adverse unless new independent refining capacity were created, and it is difficult to see how the position of the independent producer could be made any better, even if it were not made worse, without the creation of new independent refining capacity.

(2) *Rate Regulation as a Solution to the Pipe Line Problem.* Wolbert would use "cost" rates to achieve equal transportation opportunities for integrated and non-integrated companies. Rostow does not believe that this is feasible, although it would not

hurt anything and would at least be a step in the right direction. He points out that rate regulation has been tried without, in his view, any real success. The problem of "cost rates" requires further analysis, since this is not an unambiguous concept. Before proceeding with an inquiry into the nature of cost rates and their possible effectiveness in solving the pipe-line problem, it is necessary to investigate the effect of the rate regulation that has been attempted to date.

Before 1941 there was little important effort to enforce any sort of maximum rate structure on pipe lines, although there was considerable pressure for such action. However, rate regulation of a sort has been in effect since 1941, when the consent decree referred to above became applicable. Supposedly, this decree has driven rates down and has tended to relieve the allegedly exorbitant rates charged in the 1920's and 1930's. The ICC in 1948 found that the rates then in effect represented "an average decline of 17.7 cents per barrel under the rate in effect on Dec. 3, 1933, or an average rate reduction of 43.2 per cent."[54] However, as was pointed out above, the pipe-line industry in 1948 and the pipe-line industry now are two different things because of the development of mass transportation facilities. What has happened to pipe-line company profits and rates since the acceptance of the consent decree? Unfortunately, the latest data available (1953) do not reflect the full impact of the new lines, many of which were not completed until 1953; however, the figures do show the effect of increased economic activity since the beginning of the Korean War. Table 16 shows, for the period 1921 through 1953, the return on investment in carrier property (less accrued depreciation) of all pipe-line companies reporting to the ICC. The rates of return shown are the ratio of net income before and after taxes to investment in carrier property less accrued depreciation. The sample includes all companies operating in interstate commerce. The most important companies not covered are Standard of California and the Union Oil Company, which have prin-

[54] See *Reduced Pipe Line Rates and Gathering Charges,* 272 ICC 375 (1948).

TABLE 16

Return on Investment in Carrier Property of All Pipe-Line Companies Reporting to the ICC (1921–1951)

Year	Total Investment in Carrier Property	Total Investment Less Accrued Depreciation	— Net Income — Before Federal Taxes	After Federal Taxes	Return on Depreciated Investment Before Federal Taxes	After Federal Taxes
	Millions of Dollars				Per Cent	
1921	365	238	34.4	[a]	14.5	[a]
1922	382	230	58.6	[a]	25.5	[a]
1923	432	257	62.6	[a]	24.4	[a]
1924	496	291	72.2	[a]	24.8	[a]
1925	511	317	88.5	[a]	27.9	[a]
1926	539	320	80.4	[a]	25.1	[a]
1927	609	366	93.2	[a]	25.5	[a]
1928	659	385	117.2	[a]	30.4	[a]
1929	741	441	142.2	[a]	32.2	[a]
1930	773	444	123.7	[a]	27.9	[a]
1931	845	492	120.7	[a]	24.5	[a]
1932	764	428	112.4	[a]	26.3	[a]
1933	766	404	105.9	[a]	26.2	[a]
1934	758	381	104.1	84.1	27.3	22.1
1935	763	367	98.9	78.2	26.9	21.3
1936	774	372	115.1	91.7	30.9	24.7
1937	803	389	131.1	102.7	33.7	26.4
1938	808	375	117.3	92.7	31.3	24.7
1939	830	384	102.8	80.8	26.8	21.0
1940	842	384	111.6	79.9	29.1	20.8
1941	885	417	129.5	79.5	31.1	19.1
1942	919	467	110.3	56.8	23.6	12.2
1943	965	490	117.7	61.3	24.0	12.5
1944	1001	500	126.5	65.7	25.3	13.1
1945	1043	515	101.6	65.9	19.7	12.8
1946	1106	555	99.4	56.1	17.9	10.1
1947	1225	651	97.5	53.1	15.0	8.2
1948	1381	781	109.2	56.7	14.0	7.3
1949	1498	874	106.8	57.7	12.2	6.6
1950	1656	1001	163.8	81.3	16.4	8.1
1951	1822	1124	207.0	82.0	18.4	7.3
1952	2064	1329	218.6	96.6	16.4	7.3
1953	2312	1565	225.3	109.0	14.4	7.0

[a] Same as before taxes.
Sources: Computed from ICC Data published in annual *Statistics of Oil Pipe Line Companies.*

cipally intrastate pipe-line operations. The rates of return are also shown in Chart 11 (the two lower lines).

Rates of return for seven of the eight largest companies (excluding Standard of California) are shown for 1937, 1941, 1948, and 1951 in Table 17. These data do not cover all pipe lines of

Chart 11

PIPE LINE RETURN ON INVESTMENT AND TRUNK LINE RATES - ALL COMPANIES REPORTING TO THE I.C.C. (1921-1953)

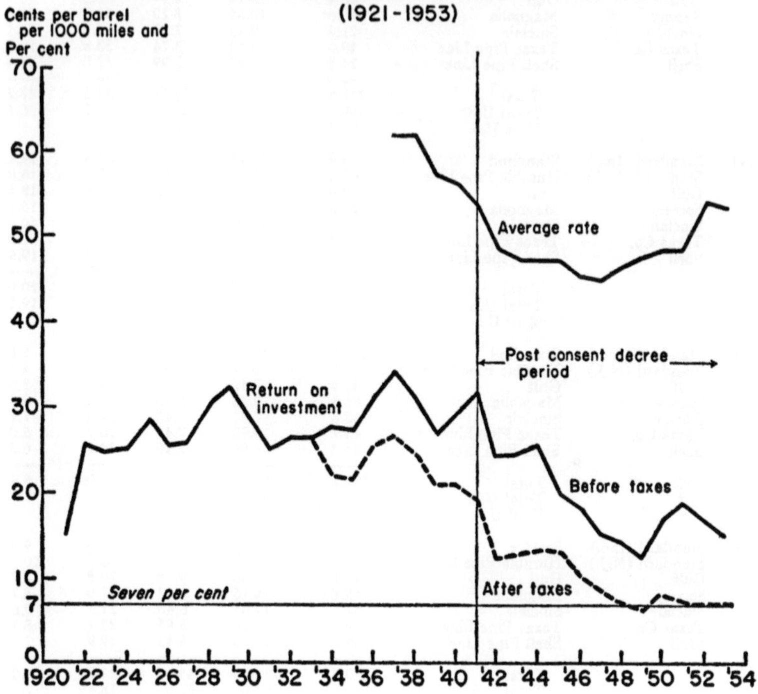

Source: Tables 16 and 18.

each company; but they are for the largest pipe-line company of each of the giant oil companies and should, therefore, be representative of these companies' pipe-line earnings.

Average realized trunk-line transportation rates (in cents per barrel per thousand miles) are shown for all companies reporting in Table 18 and Chart 11 (the top line) for the period 1937

TABLE 17

Return on Investment in Carrier Property of Principal Pipe-Line Companies of Seven Large Oil Companies (1937, 1941, 1948, and 1951)

Year	Oil Company	Pipe-Line Company	Investment Less Accrued Depreciation	— Net Income — Before Federal Taxes	After Federal Taxes	Return on Depreciated Investment Before Federal Taxes	After Federal Taxes
			Millions of Dollars			Per Cent	
1937:	Standard (Ind.)	Stanolind	38.0	12.78	9.98	33.6	26.3
	Standard (N.J.)	Humble Pipe Line	48.1	14.78	11.42	30.7	23.7
	Gulf	Gulf	40.4	13.24	12.29	32.8	30.4
	Socony	Magnolia	25.6	10.55	8.20	41.2	32.0
	Sinclair	Sinclair	21.4	9.25	7.52	43.2	35.1
	Texas Co.	Texas Pipe Line	19.6	6.63	3.74	33.8	19.1
	Shell	Shell Pipe Line	24.5	7.83	5.99	32.0	24.4
		Total	217.6	75.01	59.14	34.5	27.2
		Total U.S.	389	131.1	102.7	33.7	26.4
		% of U.S.	55.9%	57.2%	57.6%		
1941:	Standard (Ind.)	Stanolind	36.9	12.74	7.16	34.5	19.4
	Standard (N.J.)	Humble Pipe Line	41.5	11.26	6.66	27.1	16.0
	Gulf	Gulf	39.9	9.99	7.33	25.0	18.4
	Socony	Magnolia	25.0	7.38	4.52	29.5	18.1
	Sinclair	Sinclair	17.7	10.92	7.24	61.7	40.9
	Texas Co.	Texas Pipe Line	22.2	6.20	3.77	27.9	17.0
	Shell	Shell Pipe Line	21.7	7.10	4.32	32.7	19.9
		Total	204.9	65.59	41.00	32.0	20.0
		Total U.S.	417	129.5	79.5	31.1	19.1
		% of U.S.	49.1%	50.6%	51.6%		
1948:	Standard (Ind.)	Stanolind	104.0	10.22	6.02	9.8	5.8
	Standard (N.J.)	Humble Pipe Line	55.9	8.82	2.54	15.8	4.5
	Gulf	Gulf	43.4	7.42	3.75	17.1	8.6
	Socony	Magnolia	61.4	9.28	5.30	15.1	8.6
	Sinclair	Sinclair	62.8	7.81	4.45	12.4	7.1
	Texas Co.	Texas Pipe Line	48.7	4.90	2.43	10.1	5.0
	Shell	Shell Pipe Line	35.5	4.96	2.40	14.0	6.8
		Total	411.7	53.41	26.89	13.0	6.5
		Total U.S.	781	109.2	56.7	14.0	7.3
		% of U.S.	52.7%	48.9%	47.4%		
1951:	Standard (Ind.)	Service	110.5	25.22	10.32	22.8	9.3
	Standard (N.J.)	Humble Pipe Line	66.4	17.75	6.97	26.7	10.5
	Gulf	Gulf	47.1	9.82	4.18	20.8	8.9
	Socony	Magnolia	59.8	16.16	5.22	27.0	8.7
	Sinclair	Sinclair	67.6	14.67	6.48	21.7	9.6
	Texas Co.	Texas Pipe Line	70.4	16.28	5.85	23.1	8.3
	Shell	Shell Pipe Line	58.5	11.66	4.43	19.9	7.6
		Total	480.3	111.56	43.45	23.2	9.0
		Total U.S.	1124	207.0	82.0	18.4	7.3
		% of U.S.	42.7%	53.9%	53.0%		

Source: Computed from ICC Data published in annual *Statistics of Oil Pipe Line Companies.*

through 1953. These rates were computed by dividing trunk-line revenue by total barrel-miles shipped. As will be observed from the table, the rates represent crude shipments principally. The same information is shown for the seven large pipeline companies in Table 19 for the years 1937, 1941, 1948, and 1951.

TABLE 18

Average Rate for Trunk-Line Transportation of Oil — All Companies Reporting to ICC (1937–1951)

Year	Trunk Barrel-Miles Crude	Refined	Total	Trunk Line Revenue	Average Rate Cents per Bbl. per
	Billions			$000,000	1,000 Miles
1937	280.7	22.3	303.0	186.0	61.4
1938	263.1	23.7	286.8	176.1	61.4
1939	265.2	24.4	289.6	163.8	56.6
1940	282.2	23.7	305.9	171.6	56.1
1941	324.0	26.7	350.7	189.1	53.9
1942	346.1	38.4	384.5	184.4	48.0
1943	393.0	60.9	453.9	213.1	46.9
1944	437.7	70.9	508.6	239.0	47.0
1945	429.9	65.4	495.3	232.3	46.9
1946	428.8	58.8	487.6	218.7	44.9
1947	465.5	71.6	537.1	239.8	44.6
1948	513.5	85.1	598.6	273.5	45.7
1949	497.2	92.6	589.8	279.7	47.4
1950	577.1	106.6	683.7	329.2	48.1
1951	694.7	122.2	816.9	394.6	48.3
1952	714.7	142.4	857.1	461.2	53.8
1953	756.0	161.2	917.2	484.4	52.8

Source: Computed from ICC Data published in annual *Statistics of Oil Pipe Line Companies.*

It will be noted from Chart 11 that the rate of return before Federal taxes fluctuated around the 28 per cent level, more or less, with a gradually rising trend from 1922 until the institution of the consent decree. (The arithmetic mean of the rates of return for the years 1922–1941 was 28.0 per cent.) From 1941 (the year of the consent decree) to 1942 (the first year under it) the rate of return before taxes fell from 31.1 per cent to 23.6 per cent. It then rose slightly through 1944 and fell steadily to 12.2 per cent in 1949. Beginning with 1950, the rate of return before taxes turned up sharply, reaching 18.4 per cent in 1951 (41 per cent less than the 1941 level). Since 1951, this rate of return has fallen to 14.4 per cent. Data for the seven largest pipe-line companies show a similar pattern: 32.0 per cent in 1941, 13.0

TABLE 19

Average Rate for Trunk-Line Transportation of Oil — Principal Pipe-Line Companies of Seven Large Companies

Year	Oil Company	Pipe-Line Company	Trunk Barrel-Miles Billions: Crude	Refined	Total	Trunk Line Revenue $000,000	Average Rate Cents per Bbl. per 1,000 Miles
1937:	Standard (Ind.)	Stanolind	36.0	—	36.0	18.07	50.2
	Standard (N.J.)	Humble Pipe Line	32.7	—	32.7	20.80	63.6
	Gulf	Gulf	27.3	—	27.3	17.20	63.0
	Socony	Magnolia	17.5	0.2	17.7	11.76	66.4
	Sinclair	Sinclair	31.4	—	31.4	17.22	54.8
	Texas Co.	Texas Pipe Line	13.2	0.4	13.6	7.97	58.5
	Shell	Shell Pipe Line	30.0	—	30.0	15.20	50.7
		Total	188.1	0.6	188.7	108.22	57.4
		Total U.S.	280.7	22.3	303.0	186.0	61.4
		% of U.S.	67.0%	2.7%	62.2%	58.2%	
1941:	Standard (Ind.)	Stanolind	44.9	—	44.9	19.44	43.3
	Standard (N.J.)	Humble Pipe Line	32.5	—	32.5	17.55	54.0
	Gulf	Gulf	28.1	—	28.1	14.77	52.6
	Socony	Magnolia	18.3	0.5	18.8	9.82	52.2
	Sinclair	Sinclair	31.5	—	31.5	14.36	45.6
	Texas Co.	Texas Pipe Line	13.0	0.3	13.3	7.52	56.5
	Shell	Shell Pipe Line	33.8	—	33.8	13.57	40.1
		Total	202.1	0.8	202.9	97.03	47.8
		Total U.S.	324.0	26.7	350.7	189.1	53.9
		% of U.S.	62.4%	3.0%	57.9%	51.3%	
1948:	Standard (Ind.)	Stanolind	92.6	—	92.6	30.66	33.1
	Standard (N.J.)	Humble Pipe Line	45.1	1.7	46.8	25.32	54.1
	Gulf	Gulf	52.8	2.5	55.3	19.23	34.8
	Socony	Magnolia	47.3	0.7	48.0	18.11	37.7
	Sinclair	Sinclair	41.2	4.5	45.7	19.55	42.8
	Texas Co.	Texas Pipe Line	18.4	1.0	19.4	11.52	59.4
	Shell	Shell Pipe Line	35.8	1.3	37.1	13.67	36.8
		Total	333.2	11.7	344.9	138.06	40.0
		Total U.S.	513.5	85.1	598.6	273.5	45.7
		% of U.S.	64.99%	13.7%	57.6%	50.5%	
1951:	Standard (Ind.)	Service	117.5	—	117.5	45.92	39.1
	Standard (N.J.)	Humble Pipe Line	60.1	1.3	61.4	31.57	51.4
	Gulf	Gulf	50.6	2.1	52.7	20.91	39.7
	Socony	Magnolia	65.1	2.2	67.3	24.75	36.8
	Sinclair	Sinclair	48.5	9.7	58.2	33.32	57.3
	Texas Co.	Texas Pipe Line	52.7	1.8	54.5	25.01	45.9
	Shell	Shell Pipe Line	60.2	1.6	61.8	22.76	36.8
		Total	454.7	18.7	473.4	204.24	43.1
		Total U.S.	694.7	122.2	816.9	394.6	48.3
		% of U.S.	65.5%	15.3%	58.0%	51.8%	

Source: Computed from ICC Data published in annual *Statistics of Oil Pipe Line Companies.*

per cent in 1948, 23.2 per cent in 1951. The last figure is higher than that for all companies.

It may be concluded that earnings of pipe-line companies before Federal taxes are lower than before the institution of the consent decree, but that the downward trend ended, at least temporarily, in 1949. It is likely that the rate of return before Federal taxes will fluctuate around 14 or 15 per cent in the future (assuming current corporation income tax rate).

Earnings after Federal taxes followed a similar pattern until 1950. The rise in this series in that year was not appreciable, and it fell in 1951 to the 1948 level of 7.3 per cent. Earnings after taxes averaged 7.3 per cent for all companies for the period 1947 through 1953. For the large companies, earnings after taxes were 6.5 per cent in 1948 and 9.0 per cent in 1951.

It will be noted from Chart 11 that transportation rates fell from 1941 to 1942 (an accentuation of a decline from the 1937 peak), leveled, fell again, and then rose back to the 1941 level in 1952. In 1941 average rates were 53.9 cents per barrel per thousand miles; in 1953 they were 52.8 cents per barrel per thousand miles. For the large companies the rates were 47.8 cents in 1941, 40.0 cents in 1948, and 43.1 cents in 1951—a change of 4.7 cents from 1941 to 1951 (down 9.8 per cent). Since 1951, these rates have risen to about 48 cents (this figure is not precisely comparable with the earlier period).

To recapitulate: twelve years after the consent decree average transportation rates charged by all reporting companies were about the same as in 1941. The rate of return before taxes for all reporting companies decreased 53 per cent, and averaged 7.3 per cent from 1947 through 1953. In short, the net earnings of all pipe-line companies have, on the average, been driven down to the 7 per cent level. Has rate regulation, then, achieved its purpose? In a sense it has, since the high profits of the 1920's and 1930's no longer exist. This does not, however, necessarily imply that cost rates have been achieved. Furthermore, other factors than the consent decree were at work in driving down earnings. The primary responsibility seems to lie with increased Federal corporation income (and excess profit) taxes. Note that in 1953 earnings *before* such Federal taxes amounted to 14.6 per cent, compared with 7.0 per cent after taxes. Actual rates are no lower than before the consent decree, but it must be remembered that there has been an economy-wide price inflation since 1941. In terms of constant dollars, rates have fallen.

With this brief quantitative survey of the history of recent pipe-line rate regulation completed, it is now possible to proceed with the discussion of the nature of cost rates. In the beginning it will be wise to dispose of the fallacious assertion (refuted for the most part by both Rostow and Wolbert) that a payment of any kind by an independent to an integrated competitor perforce puts the independent at a competitive disadvantage.[55] The incontestable point is that someone would have to build the facility and that the builder would be entitled to a return on the money invested. As long as the independent makes no higher payment to the integrated line than he would be charged by a non-integrated line, his ability to compete is not affected by integrated ownership (apart from questions of physical access). Money paid is, after all, money paid; whether it is received by major, independent, the government, or anyone else is irrelevant.

There are, though, three valid problems involved in determining the rates to be charged in order to achieve cost rates, if this be possible (and there is some reason to doubt that it is):

(1) What is the proper rate base?
(2) What is the proper rate of return on this base?
(3) What transportation rate should be used as a basis for achieving the desired rate of return?

The problem of what the proper rate base should be is beyond the scope of this work. Whether it should be original cost less depreciation, reproduction cost, prudent investment, or something else, has been the subject of many treatises and court decisions. That it cannot be a fair *value* as a basis for a reasonable return

[55] See page 79 above. At one point, even as astute an observer as Wolbert finds it necessary to question the propriety of any payment to a competitor: "A larger question is raised whether public policy should endorse an arrangement which permits a shipper-owner to realize even a reasonable profit from carriage of his competitors' goods." (*Pipe Lines,* p. 50.) Rostow also seems to come close to this at one point: "However low the level of rates, the shipper would be forced to pay his competitor a profit on the carriage." (*National Policy,* p. 63.) Both, though, got the right answer in the end.

is, of course, apparent, since value depends on the return and hence cannot be used as a basis for the return.[56] Whatever figure is used in any particular case in the future may well be the result of bargaining between the utility board and company. For the purposes of this study, rates of return are discussed in relation to the initial dollar investment less depreciation, but one of the other criteria could be used without changing the argument as long as the same criterion is used when discussing the costs of both majors and independents.

It is in order, however, to examine the proper size of the *return* on the investment, however the latter may be computed, and to present the problem involved in choosing a rate which will give this return. A cost rate, as advocated by Wolbert, would apparently equal the sum of variable costs (those expenditures which fluctuate with output, for example, electric power) and fixed costs (cost variant with time, for example, depreciation, labor, taxes, interest, and so forth). Fixed costs would include an "opportunity" cost representing a return on the investment. Ascertaining the appropriate cash costs is a relatively straightforward, if not a simple, process (see Chapter I); but "opportunity cost" is a matter of some controversy.

Opportunity cost is the foregone gain which a firm incurs by putting its money in one industry, for example, pipe lines, instead of in some other income-earning endeavor. Had the firm put its money in a riskless investment (government bonds), it could have earned 3 per cent per year (before income taxes). Consequently, at least this much is a cost of entering *any* business. An opportunity cost should ordinarily be applied even to *borrowed* funds if they are invested in one industry when they could have been invested elsewhere at a higher return. This is necessary because there is a foregone gain equal to the difference between the sacrificed return and the return available in the industry chosen.

Furthermore, the oil company might have been able to earn 25 per cent on money put into new oil wells instead of into pipe lines. The extra 22 percentage points might also be considered

[56] See *Federal Power Commission* vs. *Hope Natural Gas Co.*, 320 U.S. 591, 601.

an "opportunity cost" of putting funds into the pipe line. However, in this case it is the "net" opportunity cost (one is tempted to call it a "marginal" opportunity cost) which is relevant. The firm might be able potentially to earn 25 per cent in crude production, but this would only be possible if there were pipe-line capacity to get the crude out of the fields. If no one else will build this capacity, then the oil company may either build its own line or leave the field undeveloped. Consequently it must take into account the potential loss from not having the production when ascertaining the opportunity cost for the pipe-line funds; under these conditions, the (marginal) pipe-line opportunity cost might well be quite low. Indeed, if the firm provided the funds to build its own pipe line, it might be justified in using a zero marginal opportunity cost. The actual cost of building the line (variable costs, depreciation, taxes, and other expenses) is probably sufficient — since there is no real alternative use of these funds if the firm is to operate the rest of its vertically integrated enterprise.

On the other hand, the opportunity cost on funds used to build pipe-line capacity for *others* might well be high — because this represents an expenditure which is necessary only because of the Hepburn Act and which could otherwise be made elsewhere in the oil industry, or in some other profitable industry, should the company so choose. An acceptable figure in this case might be the rate of return which the company could expect on its whole integrated operation. (This, by the way, is the only average earning figure which has any real meaning, since vertical integration is necessary — given the current structure of the industry — for the large companies to be able to operate at all.) Even this generalization might not hold true if some oil company could have earned even higher returns in some other business. It is hardly necessary to add that opportunity cost will vary from firm to firm above the 3 per cent minimum, depending on the opportunities each firm could have realized.

What is the proper opportunity cost rate for an oil company on pipe-line facilities built for others? One negative statement may be made. There is no a priori reason to expect the proper cost-rate return on investment in pipe-line facilities for others to be, as Rostow apparently considers it, a "long-run normative return," if by a long-run normative return is meant something slightly more than the return available in a riskless investment, for example, about 4 per cent. In 1951, the large pipe-line companies (see Table 17) netted 9.0 per cent after taxes from earnings of 23.2 per cent before taxes; all companies earned 7.3 per cent after taxes from earnings of 18.4 per cent before. This is a far cry from Rostow's "long-run normative return," and it is in all probability above the opportunity cost to an integrated oil company of building its own pipe-line facilities.

Is it, though, above the cost of building pipe lines for other people? It might well not be. In 1951, the year these companies averaged 23.2 per cent before taxes and 9.0 per cent after taxes on pipe-line operations, their total company-wide earnings averaged 10.3 per cent after taxes (see Table 20). This is somewhat

TABLE 20

Rate of Return of Seven Large Oil Companies (1951)

Company	Total Assets Less Depreciation	Net Income: Before Income Taxes	Net Income: After Income Taxes	Rate of Return: Before	Rate of Return: After
	(000,000's)			Per Cent	
Standard (N.J.)	$ 4707.0	$ 931.1	$ 528.5	19.8	11.2
Standard (Ind.)	1800.5	247.7	148.7	13.8	8.3
Socony-Vacuum	1792.5	249.6	161.6	13.9	9.0
Texas Co.	1549.4	261.4	178.8	16.9	11.5
Gulf	1511.6	239.2	140.0	15.8	9.3
Sinclair	880.0	119.1	81.9	13.5	9.3
Shell	792.2	205.1	97.0	25.9	12.2
All Seven	$13,033.2	$2253.2	$1336.5	17.3%	10.3%

Source: Computed from information in Moody's *Industrials.*

more than the pipe-line earnings (which are double-taxed to the extent of 15 per cent when declared as dividends from subsidiaries, thereby making pipe-line profit dollars worth less than other profit dollars). Consequently, the major companies in 1951 would have had considerable justification under a program of "cost rates" for charging pipe-line rates on outside shipments high enough to yield a 10 per cent return (after income taxes) on funds invested in such shipments — a rate of earning equaled by only one large pipe-line company in 1951. Such a return would imply rates high enough to give a return of perhaps 26 per cent before taxes, on the basis of this company's experience under the 1951 tax structure, or about 20 per cent before taxes under current tax rates. (Even the 10 per cent return on over-all operations is understated to some extent, since it was held down somewhat by pipe-line earnings subject to the 7 per cent regulation.)

Although 10 per cent returns after taxes can be justified as "cost" by the major, it is doubtful indeed whether independent refiners would consider such rates ostensibly designed to provide equal transportation opportunities to be a boon to their business — especially if the "cost rates" were higher than current rates (7.0 per cent after taxes in 1953).

Since opportunity cost varies from company to company, and since it is a hypothetical quantity in any event, it is impossible to state precisely what the proper figure should be on any one non-integrated refiner's own funds; but it would, like the majors', be low for a pipe line required before the refinery could be operated. If the funds were borrowed, an acceptable figure for the true cost to the independent of providing his own pipe-line facilities might be the variable costs, taxes, depreciation, and the appropriate rate of interest with no extra opportunity cost. This covers the cash outlays of the independent and is in accord with the "marginal" cost to the larger company of providing itself with pipe-line service (discussed above). It is safe to say that either the opportunity or interest cost to the independent of providing his own transportation would be something less than the return of over 20 per cent which he must pay the major in order that the major may get back *his* cost of providing the pipe-line service for the independent, at least in the case of a going concern.

To a *potential* independent refiner, the incremental opportunity cost of adding transport capacity to a planned refinery expenditure would also be the actual rate of interest on the extra funds unless the necessity of building the pipe line in turn necessitated a decrease in the size of the refinery because of a limit on the amount of capital available. In this event the cost to the potential independent refiner would include the foregone gain from operating a smaller refinery — a business which will likely yield lower returns than those earned by integrated companies, given current prices of crude and products. For either the existing or potential independent, however, the foregone gain would probably be considerably less than 20 per cent before taxes.

If a lower percentage were accepted for "cost rates," as it must be if current competitive conditions are to be equalized by equalizing costs under Wolbert's proposed policy, then the rates might have to be set to make the pipe line break even (if it were built with funds borrowed at the same interest available to the independents). Some extra return might be allowed to the company building the line for the risk it assumed which was not assumed by the independents, but rates yielding any higher returns would involve the independents in payments greater than "cost." Such rates under Hepburn Act regulation would force anyone building a pipe line to (1) build sufficient capacity for all others who might desire to use the line and (2) charge a rate which would cover only the marginal cost that the others would have incurred had they built their own lines. In other words, the pipe-line builder would be forced to use his money (or borrowed funds) which he could have used for other purposes to build pipe-line facilities for other people — not at the return he could have earned elsewhere, but at the lower marginal cost of providing one's own facilities. Such a system of rates allowing no profits would constitute a pronounced departure from traditional public-utility regulation.

What kind of "cost rates" does Wolbert actually envisage? In the first place, he would abandon the consent decree and return pipe-line rate regulation to the ICC "where it rightfully belongs."

He would apparently require the ICC to set "reasonable" cost rates covering cash costs and a return on the investment. He notes that ICC rulings prescribe 8 per cent as the reasonable limit for any given line and cites the average return at the time of his writing (8.3 per cent) as "a reasonable transportation expense to shippers and a reasonable return for the pipe line proprietors." [57] Note that this is 8.3 per cent *after* Federal taxes. Consequently, it must be concluded that Wolbert would be satisfied with common-carrier regulation requiring integrated companies to build pipe-line capacity for others at a return of about 8 per cent *after* taxes. This is a system like that in use, except that it would be administered by a different agency without the alleged ambiguities of the consent decree. It would permit rates which yield earnings amounting to some 20 per cent before taxes. This return would be just from the majors' point of view, since they are forced to provide pipe-line facilities for others with money they could have used elsewhere. It is, however, much higher than the return which would equalize competitive conditions for non-integrated companies. It is difficult to see how such regulation satisfies anyone; the major is forced to build pipe-line capacity he might not want to build and the independent does not get "cost" transportation (from his point of view).

In the matter of requiring anyone building a pipe line to operate it as a common carrier, Wolbert apparently disapproves of the denial of the private-carrier concept to oil companies: "The private carrier concept is well established in both the motor carrier and water carrier fields. There seems to be no valid reason why it should be excluded from the pipe line area." [58]

However, in his recommendation that rate regulation be given back to the ICC, he does not suggest the concurrent removal of ratable-taking powers; he, in fact, speaks of these powers approvingly. Indeed, the very fact that he advocates public-utility regulation of the existing lines at cost rates indicates that he must approve of their status as common carriers under the Hepburn

[57] Wolbert, *Pipe Lines*, p. 21.
[58] *Pipe Lines*, p. 131.

Act. Otherwise, even though cost rates were charged, the independents would have no guaranteed access to the lines. Hence there would be no guarantee of equalized competitive conditions. It must be concluded, then, that Wolbert would approve of continued enforced common-carrier status of the existing lines. If not, his policy would not equalize competitive conditions unless independent common carriers were to appear; Wolbert considers this to be most unlikely.

Furthermore, this writer agrees with Rostow that public-utility regulation is by its very nature incapable of achieving *any* precise return on investment — apart from the common public-utility problems of deciding what the "investment" is, what the return should be, and so forth. There need only be an increase in pipe-line volume for a predetermined transportation rate set as "fair" to become too high — yielding exorbitant rates of return resulting from the action of neither an inefficient public-utility board nor a monopolistic oil company, but merely from an unexpected advance in the demand for petroleum products. Observe in Tables 17 and 19 what happened to earnings and rates of the large companies from 1948 to 1951. Earnings increased from 13.0 per cent to 23.2 per cent (up 78 per cent). Absolute net income rose from 53.4 to 111.6 million dollars — up 109 per cent. Rates, though, rose only from 40.0 to 43.1 cents per barrel per thousand miles — an increase of only 8 per cent. What explains the rise in earnings? Certainly not monopolistic rate increases alone, or even primarily. The total barrel-miles carried by these companies rose from 344.9 billion to 473.4 billion — an increase of 37 per cent. Volume increases, then, were much more important than rate increases. (These together account for only a 48 per cent rise in absolute earnings, leaving another 61 percentage points which may be attributed to decreasing costs per barrel with increased throughput and to the use of cheaper mass transportation.) This is a perfect example of the inappropriateness of rate regulation in setting a given level of return, even if the amount of the investment and the rate of return were matters of no dispute whatever. It is almost impossible to choose a transportation rate in advance that will guarantee any desired level of earnings.

Wolbert's proposal of "cost" rates, then, is in this writer's opinion deficient, since it is subject to four basic criticisms: (1) public utility regulation, as a decade of it bears out, cannot be that precise; (2) "cost rates," from the point of view of the major, would not be any lower than current rates (higher, if anything), and hence would change nothing; (3) "cost rates" from the point of view of the independent would be lower than the return to which the major is entitled; and (4) the Hepburn Act provision denying private carrier privileges to the oil companies would be continued.

(3) *Divorcement as a Solution to the Pipe-Line Problem.* Cost rates, then, are rejected as a means of providing equal transportation opportunities for all. What would be the effects of divorcement of the pipe lines? In considering the effect of divorcement it will be necessary to distinguish between the effects on existing pipe lines and refineries and on new pipe lines and refineries.

(a) *Existing pipe lines.* Wolbert cited two cases of independent pipe lines which did not fare well. However, one of these is not an appropriate example for discussing existing lines. The Prairie pipe-line system was divorced from an integrated company, but Crusader was built as an independent line from an oil field to a river. As such it is not a parallel case to any existing crude oil pipe line. Furthermore, there are other systems which survived the dissolution of the old Standard Oil Company and still operate. There is insufficient evidence from actual cases to indicate what would happen to existing pipe lines if they were divorced. Furthermore, as Rostow pointed out, actual evidence would be of doubtful value, since any past independent pipe lines would have had to compete with integrated pipe lines. Rostow's other reply to this proposition, viz., that independent natural gas pipe lines operate successfully, is invalid. The existing interstate gas pipelines are not by any means common carriers. They *buy* gas and transmit it for resale. The independent crude oil pipe lines which might be created by dis-integration would have to be common carriers. Otherwise they could exert a vertical integration squeeze by use of their monopsony position relative to producers and their monopoly position relative to refiners. By refusing to carry any oil but their own, they could effectively control the price of crude.

It would appear to this observer that there is no reason why an existing line that is part of an integrated operation would not continue in business as successfully after divorcement as before — until, of course, the crude sources it serves become uneconomical. This is a risk faced by any pipe line, independent or integrated. As long, however, as the refineries and fields which it served before divorcement continue to operate, the line should also continue to operate. To the extent that they are operating at capacity, there is, indeed, little reason to believe that the existing lines would even experience much of a change in customers. Should new independent refining capacity be encouraged by divorcement, then the lines might have to carry somewhat less oil (as common carriers giving proportional shipments) for their present customers; otherwise, nothing should change, at least insofar as the volume of operations is concerned.

Once the fields served by an independent line begin to diminish and become marginal, then the line would be at a disadvantage if it were not permitted to discriminate in rates in favor of marginal producers. Remember that an *integrated* line would not have to discriminate. Only in this case should an integrated line have any advantage over a dis-integrated line. Note that these are divorced lines, not *new* independent lines.

There is some possibility that newly divorced lines might demand higher rates than those now charged. Wolbert believes that this would be the case. Rostow does not refute this contention. Wolbert's reason is that the independent pipe-line owner would be apt to seek higher rates, since his sole interest is in making a pipe-line profit — while that of the integrated company is to obtain a continuous supply of crude for the refinery. This assertion would be theoretically indefensible if there were no government regulations of rates. An oil company, like any free enterprise, is in business to make money; consequently, it should maximize its pipe-line profits on outside shipments. If it were rational for an independent pipe line to raise rates, that is, if there would be a net increase in total profit thereafter, then it would also have been rational for an integrated line to raise the rates — *if* there were no government regulation. However, it may well not be worth an integrated company's time and effort to try to pry higher rates out of two government agencies. The only desirable effect would be increased profits on the small amount of oil carried for others. Profits on its own oil, the bulk of its shipments, come from the whole integrated operation, regardless of where they appear on the books. The small increase in total revenue accruing from an increase in rates on outside shipments would hardly justify an effort to have the consent decree set aside. Furthermore, increasing pipe-line rates would shift part of the profits on the company's own oil to the pipe-line stage of the company. As was noted previously, it might be unwise to shift profits from the parent company to a pipe-line subsidiary, since 15 per cent of the dividends paid would be subject to double taxation. It is quite possible that this might offset any increased revenue from outsiders (especially in companies where pipe-line companies are subsidiaries of subsidiaries).

On the other hand, a divorced line which is solely dependent on pipe-line revenues would have an extra incentive to try to get higher rates. The reason for this is that the higher rates would affect its profits on *all* oil shipped, not on a minor part of total throughput. Should higher rates result, the few independent refiners who now use the crude line of majors would suffer from divorcement, as would the majors (unless their "cost" were less than current rates — unlikely on their own shipments).

(b) *Existing refineries.* Can divorcement solve the competitive problems (if any) of existing refineries? For example, would the removal of this "control" device assist in alleviating such a problem as that which existed in the East Texas field in the late 1930's? In the TNEC *Hearings*[59] it was stated that the number

[59] TNEC *Hearings,* Part 15, p. 8538.

of independent refineries decreased from 74 to three in the period 1935–1941. At least 26 of these were supposedly modern plants.[60] Would independent pipe-line ownership have solved or helped solve such a problem?

The answer is clear: divorcement in 1935 would not have materially helped these 26 plants because they were crude-oriented refineries, probably serving local markets. Nor would divorcement materially aid most independent refining capacity, since 52 per cent of all independent refining capacity is principally crude-oriented (see Table 5). Another 28 per cent is located in the Gulf Coast and Los Angeles Basin areas which are principally nodal and major market areas respectively, but are also areas where there are crude supplies, giving a total of 80 per cent located near crude supplies. Table 6 indicates that on the basis of location alone only 48 per cent of independent refining capacity, including that in the Gulf Coast and Los Angeles areas, could be affected by pipe-line divorcement. The figure of 48 per cent is a maximum based on location alone (as will be shown below, the correct figure is actually much smaller). This 48 per cent of independent capacity represents only 10 per cent of total United States capacity. Government legislative or judicial action to aid such a proportion of existing plants might, with some validity, be called "special interest" action.

The refineries represented in the 48 per cent must now be examined further by areas and by plants (for the larger plants at least). In the first place, the capacity in the Los Angeles Basin can in part at least be eliminated as a market for trunk-line crude oil. According to Professor Bain, from 40 per cent to 50 per cent of the oil produced in the Los Angeles Basin in the early 1940's was purchased by independent refiners.[61] Transportation was not a problem for these independents. There are some independently owned gathering systems. More important, distances are short and truck transportation can be used without incurring serious cost disadvantages.

[60] There are about eight independent refineries in East Texas now.
[61] J. S. Bain, *Pacific Coast Petroleum Industry,* part i, p. 55.

Although control of transport facilities on the Pacific Coast is similarly concentrated relative to the Mid-Continent the fact that the principal market and refining area is contiguous to the chief producing area, and that distances to other fields are relatively short . . . make it unlikely that a pipe line squeeze will develop here.[62]

Forty per cent of the current MER producing capacity in the Los Angeles Basin is 140,000 barrels per day (see Table 12); active independent refining capacity in this area amounts to about 100,000 barrels per day. Hence, although total refining capacity in this area outstrips total producing capacity, it would appear that independents can buy a sufficiently large share to avoid dependency on San Joaquin Valley crude. On the other hand, Professor Bain's data were collected in 1941–1942; since that time an oil shortage has developed in California, and it is only reasonable to expect that the independents are affected as well as the majors. However, Canadian oil to be supplied to the Pacific Northwest (through the new pipe line from Alberta) will relieve the pressure on California crude, thereby making California's production available solely for use in California. This is expected to make California self-sufficient in crude production for the present at least.

Next, the refineries at Corpus Christi, Texas can be eliminated, at least as markets for large crude trunk lines (there is a small line from West Texas). These refineries are located near large fields. The MER for the South Gulf Coast is greater by far than the independent refining capacity in this area.

In Central Michigan (not included in Table 6) an approximation to that part of independent refining capacity which constitutes a market for pipe lines can be made by substracting MER production capacity (37,000 barrels per day) from total refining capacity (93,000 barrels per day), giving a total "import" of 56,000 barrels per day. Since 95 per cent of the area refining capacity is independent, this figure is probably acceptable as an

[62] Bain, pp. 82–83.

indicator of the potential market there. (To the extent that there is cross hauling, that is, to the extent that Michigan crude is exported, this figure understates the requirements.)

Now we may examine the large plants outside of these three regions, including the crude-oriented refineries which might be customers for the services of products lines. Those covered will include all plants having capacities of 25,000 barrels per day or more. First, the Ashland Refining Company plant at Cattlesburg, Kentucky. This plant draws on crude from the Eastern Kentucky field (with its own pipe-line connections) and from the South with its own barges.[63] It is probably valid to assume that much of the rest of the Ashland "empire" also has either its own barge or gathering transportation. This is, after all, an integrated, expanding company.

Second, the refineries near Houston. The largest is Republic Oil Company at Texas City, Texas. This 70,000-barrel-per-day refinery might have been an ideal test case for divorcement, since it belongs to the Plymouth Oil Company, an important independent crude producer. Would it have prospered more with free access to pipe lines, together with the existing access to crude in the fields? Unfortunately, it too has become an integrated company. It holds a share in the current Rancho pipe line being built from West Texas to Houston by Shell as a joint venture among Shell and several other companies, major and independent: Shell; Pan American, a subsidiary of Standard (Indiana); Sinclair; Phillips; Republic; Eastern States; and Crown Central (see Table 2). This line together with local crude supplies on the Gulf Coast should leave these three independents — Republic, Eastern States, and Crown-Central — relatively free of major domination, particularly since they have tidewater facilities permitting crude imports.

Third, Sunray's plants in Oklahoma (crude-oriented) are served by crude gathering lines, a 6-inch products line connecting the Duncan plant to the Allen plant, and an 8-inch products

[63] Rostow and Sachs, "Entry," p. 89.

line connecting the Allen plant to the Great Lakes products system.[64]

Fourth, Mid-Continent petroleum is an integrated oil company; it is crude-oriented, has 1741 miles of gathering lines, 1274 tank cars, and owns a 19 per cent interest in the Great Lakes system.[65]

The Gilmore Refineries' projected plant in West Texas (crude-oriented) will not be a market for products lines, if it is built, since it plans to build its own line to the West Coast in order to sell its products in that area.[66]

One independent plant operating on common carrier crude at the present is the Globe Refining Company at Chicago;[67] since it is using existing lines, it could hardly constitute a new market upon divorcement. (This plant is indicated under "Mid-West Refining Company" in Chapter II since it is a subsidiary of that company; that company's other plant at Alma, Michigan, is apparently served by the Michigan-Ohio Pipe Line Company in which Mid-West holds a 75 per cent interest.)

Without pausing to examine the plants having capacities less than 25,000 barrels per day, the pattern of independent reliance on crude pipe-line transportation should be fairly clear. One is tempted to say, "Enough of the traditional concept of 'independent' and 'major.' " What really matters is *integrated* and *non*-integrated. Of the latter, there are very few companies indeed having non-crude-oriented refineries of any size. This elimination has accounted for all but four of the plants in the United States (outside the Los Angeles area) which have a capacity of 25,000 barrels per day or more. Apparently no published data are available on three of them (Texas City Refining, Aurora, and Sid Richardson). The other is Great Northern at St. Paul. Here is a case of an expansion of a small, market-oriented refinery from 5000 to 30,000 barrels per day when independent pipe-line ca-

[64] Information on Sunray, Mid-Continent, Globe, and Mid-West from Moody's *Industrials*. Other data from private sources.

[65] Moody's *Industrials*.

[66] As of November 1954, this plan had not been carried out.

[67] Rostow and Sachs, "Entry," p. 89.

pacity is built; however, it will not constitute a new, untapped market for crude lines should they be divorced.

Even if none of the remaining capacity in Table 6 has its own transportation facilities, the total capacity of remaining plants which have a plant capacity of 10,000 barrels per day or more (Los Angeles excluded) is only about 200,000 barrels per day, or 11.6 per cent of independent refining capacity and 2.4 per cent of total refining capacity. The other independent capacity (Los Angeles excluded) which might use crude lines is made up of plants having less than 7500 barrels per day each—most of which even Professor Rostow's cost data[68] would probably put beneath the minimum efficiency mark. The total capacity of both large and small independents which are not crude-oriented and which have no identified transportation facilities (including the appropriate capacity in Central Michigan) accounts for 29 per cent of independent capacity and 6 per cent of total capacity. Of this, 144,000 barrels per day (8.4 per cent of independent capacity) are in local market areas where large lines would be uneconomic.

It may be concluded that only a small part of existing independent capacity, perhaps 20 per cent including the very small refineries, could be materially assisted by divorcement of crude pipe lines. This is only 4 per cent of total refining capacity. Efficient independent refining capacity (by the most charitable definition of "efficient capacity") which could be assisted by divorcement of pipe lines amounts to only 2.4 per cent of total United States refining capacity. These measures are not precise, of course, but they should be close to the actual figure. There are two possible errors which might be of importance, but these tend to offset each other. First, since all these plants are operating at some fraction of their total capacity, they are probably getting some crude from the major's pipe lines; hence, there is some overstatement. Conversely, there may well be some offsetting understatement in that all of the plants eliminated from the tabulation in Table 7 may not utilize pipe-line facilities to the full

[68] See page 92.

extent of their capacity (substituting rail, truck, or barge shipments) or may not be operating at capacity because of a lack of access to crude.

(c) *New independent refineries.* It has been shown that rate regulation is not a promising means of achieving equal transportation opportunities. Furthermore, divorcement of pipe lines would not materially affect either existing pipe lines or existing independent refineries. The case for divorcement, therefore, rests solely on the impetus that would be given to well-located new independent refining capacity. Furthermore, this writer would add a qualification. Not only must well-located new independent refining capacity be created, this new capacity must be sufficiently large and efficient to increase effective competition in the gasoline and other refined products markets. To those who believe, as does Professor Rostow, that "perhaps the most important reason" for industrial reorganization by government action is the re-creation of a society of small economic units,[69] this is not a necessary qualification. Conceding that an economy of small units might well be politically and socially desirable (as long as there is no great economic cost involved in achieving it), this observer must admit that he is more interested in the effect that any proposed public policies toward pipe lines might have on the price of gasoline.

Entry into the refining business can be promoted by divorcement of the pipe lines only if such entry is relatively free, excepting major company ownership of the pipe lines. If this ownership were removed by divorcement folowed by enforced common carrier status for the lines, then potential independent refiners would have access to independent crude supplies (to the extent that their oil could be carried in the lines under ratable takings). If denial of this access, either actual or potential denial,

[69] "Industrial organization has sociological and political results. One of the major problems requiring a social decision in our time is whether we could achieve a wider dispersal of power and opportunity, and a broader base for the class structure of our society, by a more competitive organization of this and other industries, in smaller and more independent units." Rostow, *A National Policy for the Oil Industry,* p. xii.

by pipe-line ownership has been the majors' "chief weapon" of market control in the past, then new independent refineries might well spring up at market centers in the event of divorcement.

What *are* the factors affecting freedom of entry into refining? Basically, of course, profit expectations would have to be sufficient to justify the initial investment cost. What would determine these expectations, outside of the usual aggregative business outlook and specific forecasts of petroleum demand? The relative prices of crude oil, including transportation costs, and refined products; the degree of dominance the majors would retain over the crude and gasoline markets (and also other refined products, of course); the cost disadvantages, if any, a new small firm would encounter relative to existing large firms; the chance of construction of new pipe lines, or in their absence, the chance of obtaining space in existing lines; the ease of obtaining rights to the use of modern processes; and so forth — these are the determinants of business opportunity in petroleum refining. Furthermore, the absolute size of the investment might be of significance in determining freedom of entry. If very large sums of capital were required, then regardless of the rosiness of the profit outlook, entry might be difficult; the capital market is not, after all, perfect. While it is not the purpose of this inquiry to investigate the costs of petroleum refining, some idea of the initial outlay required can be had from the following data: of nineteen projects under way early in 1953 to build new small refineries or expand the crude input capacities of existing refineries, the range of initial cost per barrel of capacity per day was \$326 to \$1200; the mean was \$845.[70] The wide range of costs per barrel per day could be explained by many things, for example, various types of plants, poor estimates, erroneous reporting, and so forth. The figures, however, give some idea of the general magnitudes of the capital outlays necessary. A 25,000-barrel refinery might be expected to cost some \$21.1 million initially.

None of these problems has been adequately investigated by

[70] Computed from information in *Petroleum Refiner* "Boxscores," 1952 issues.

the proponents of divorcement. Refining cost functions would shed, at the very least, negative light on the problem. The evidence presented by Rostow and Sachs is not convincing. It is at least as subject to criticism of "tantalizingly brief" as that of Wolbert to the contrary. It would hardly be expected that small independent refiners would admit their plants to be inefficient.[71] If the refinery district where 17,500 barrels per day is the minimum efficient size contains giant refineries (for example, 200,000 barrels per day) with which the small plants must compete, then economies of scale may well not be important in refining. On the other hand, if all competing refineries in the given district are small, no such conclusion can be drawn. The engineering estimate is well taken, if "Mid-Continent" does not mean simply Oklahoma and Kansas, where there are no giant refineries. If "well-located" Mid-Continent implies near the centers at Chicago or St. Louis, then this would be a valid bit of evidence indicating that relatively small refineries approach the efficiency of the very large ones. There is another more explicit bit of evidence which places the "minimum efficient" size at 30,000 barrels per day and the most efficient over 200,000. If Dr. Wilson in "Is Big Business Bad?" should be right, then minimum costs would not begin to be reached until capacity reached, say, 100,000 barrels per day. (This figure is computed by using "three" for "several" as a minimum and multiplying by 30,000.) A substantial percentage of refining capacity is accounted for by plants of this size or larger — 45 per cent according to Table 10.

Refinery cost curves are beyond the scope of this study, but a word or two may be injected here. Although there is no technological reason for expecting capital economies of scale in the construction of fractionating towers (for crude oil), since the wall thickness of the tower must be increased as its capacity is increased, one company is now building a 125,000-barrel-per-day (single unit) fractionating tower. Would it do this instead of building, say, eight such towers if the operating expenses on a single unit were greater than on eight smaller units? In addition,

[71] See the quotation on page 92 above.

there *are* technological reasons for expecting capital economies of scale in one of the most important units of a modern refinery: the catalytic cracker. There are two principal reasons for this: (1) that crackers require large amounts of auxiliary facilities (tankage, piping, and so forth) regardless of size; and (2) that there are economies of scale obtained from the retention of heat in large vessels. A catalytic cracker requires an expensive lining

Chart 12

INITIAL COSTS PER BARREL OF OUTPUT – FLUID CATALYTIC CRACKERS

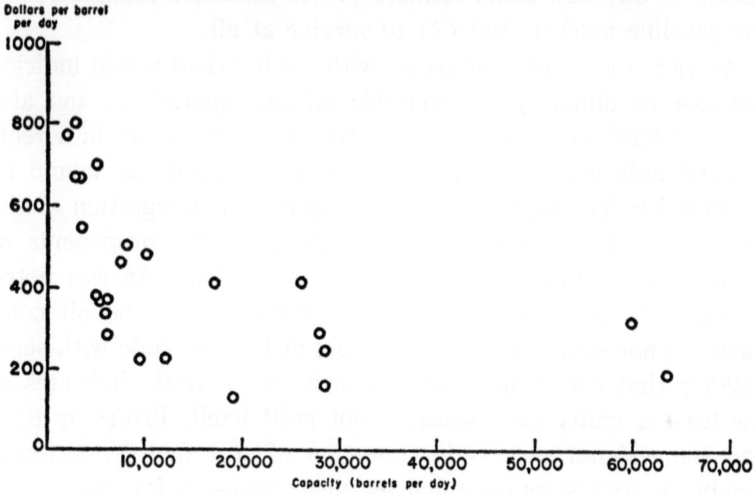

Source: Tabulated from *Petroleum Refiner* "Boxscores" and private sources.

in its reactor; a large reactor gets more lining per unit of volume than a small (for similar reasons to those set out above for pipeline volume versus surface area). These capital economies of scale in building catalytic crackers are illustrated in Chart 12 which shows dollars of initial cost per barrel of capacity plotted against capacity. Furthermore, if one unit of a refinery has capital economies of scale in its construction, then for "balance" the rest of the refinery must be large also — unless it can be shown to exhibit increasing average costs with size, something which has not been contended even by the most vigorous advocates of disintegration. Finally, large refineries can afford to make minor products, especially lubricants, which may be the difference between prosperity and bankruptcy, since they are minor in volume but not in revenue-producing ability.

Should cost curves show constant average costs from, say, 15,000 to 150,000 barrels per day, this would be evidence that new small refineries can compete cost-wise. Whether other factors might preclude active competition on their part would not, of course, be disclosed. Should such a study disclose decreasing average costs, then serious questions would be raised concerning the ability of any new small refiners (1) to influence competition in the gasoline market, and (2) to survive at all.

Average total costs compared with crude prices would indicate the ease or difficulty of profitable refining operations, and also the likelihood of gasoline price increases or decreases in a reorganized industry. It is essential that these questions should be answered before engaging in a widespread dis-integration of the industry. It is not necessarily a criticism of the proponents of dis-integration that the problems are not solved. As was noted above, obtaining the necessary information from the oil companies is not easy. Perhaps professors of law conclude with some validity that concealment of evidence, so to speak, indicates at the least a guilty conscience, if not guilt itself. Professor Bain had some signal success in collection of cost figures; unfortunately his data were compiled ten years ago — before the extensive introduction of the most important recent innovation in refining, catalytic cracking. The same limitation applies to the few scattered facts in the TNEC *Hearings*. Even when the data are made available there are difficult problems of analysis and comparability. It is to be hoped that several of the current large-scale studies of vertical integration will produce refining cost curves. The monumental work by Professors McLean and Haigh (which appeared after the completion of this monograph) has refining cost curves for the operation as a whole which show decreasing costs, similar to those in Chart 12.[72]

[72] See McLean and Haigh, *The Growth of the Integrated Oil Companies*, chapter xx, especially p. 561.

Even if new, independent refining capacity were created by a divorcement of pipe lines, would effective competition (not "pure" competition), necessarily be enhanced? Would an increase in independent refinery capacity from 1720 thousand barrels per day to 2500 or 2550 thousand barrels per day (that is, to approximately the level of independent crude production) mean an end to the oligopolistic conditions supposedly present in most local gasoline markets? Even with free entry cost-wise in an industry, there is no necessary reason to expect any greater degree of competition should this free entry be permitted to operate. The existing companies in any industry may well be able to maintain their dominance over the market for a multitude of other reasons than cost advantages — for example, (1) existing consumer good will, (2) the acceptance by small companies of a policy of "live and let live" in order to avoid the dangers of vigorous retaliatory price competition by financially powerful giant companies, (3) the necessity of creating sales organizations equipped to compete with the existing companies, and so forth. There is no certainty that these apply in the oil industry; but to the extent that they do, effective competition would not be enhanced by the entry of new refining companies.

In sum, then, the economic case for pipe-line divorcement, insofar as refineries are concerned, may be said to stand on the (unknown) degree of freedom of entry into refining which would be created, and the (unknown) extent of effective new competition which would be occasioned by such entry. In this writer's view it is only by demonstrating that divorcement would appreciably assist those independents large enough to promote more vigorous price competition in the refined markets market that a program of dis-integration can be justified — especially when such a program carries with it the danger of higher transportation costs. This demonstration has not yet adequately been made by the proponents of divorcement. Indeed, the cost data of McLean and Haigh indicate that new plants must be large to compete with large plants. No attempt will be made here to investigate the problem further since it is the belief of this writer that there is a much better solution than dis-integration — one which carries none of its dangers and still provides for its alleged advantages.

(d) *New pipe lines.* Before turning to an examination of this solution, one final point must be summarized, namely, the prospects for new independent pipe lines or the expansion of newly created independent lines in the event of the adoption of a public policy which forbids integrated lines. To some extent, as Wolbert points out, such prospects depend on the prospects of new independent refineries. New independent refineries would mean more business for new independent pipe lines; on the other hand, new independent pipe-line capacity may be a prerequisite to the building of new refineries. Which came first, the acorn or the oak? If it were established that entry is relatively easy into refining and that the only existing barrier thereto is major company ownership of pipe lines, then it might not be unreasonable to expect expansions of existing lines (by adding stations), even should the laying of completely new lines be unlikely. However, since we know so little about the problems of entry faced by independent refiners (and since part of the available cost material indicates that these problems are considerable), we cannot justifiably conclude that independent pipe-line companies would help create independent refining capacity, and thereby enhance their own business, simply by providing transportation facilities. Until the other questions on entry are fully answered, this one cannot be.

A more important question involved the willingness of independent pipe-line companies to provide service to new fields, as opposed to new refineries. As was pointed out above, Rostow and Sachs apparently have two opinions on how eager independents would be to expand old lines to new fields or to build completely new ones.[73] On the one hand, they imply "less eager" than integrated companies; on the other hand, they imply "more eager." Wolbert would say "considerably less eager." One other remark from Rostow and Sachs might serve to confuse the picture somewhat more, or perhaps to clarify it. They state that it is an "unquestioned fact" that "pipe line construction is inherently haz-

[73] See Rostow and Sachs, "Entry," p. 896.

ardous." Why? "While the great lines serving large consuming markets are reasonably sure of traffic, gathering lines to particular fields, or trunk lines based on a flow from particular areas are not." [74] This point is not questioned in the subsequent discussion. With this viewpoint the writer is inclined to agree wholeheartedly, especially if the trunk line is to be an efficient one. The likelihood of finding an independent company which would be willing to spend, say, $100 million to bring oil 1000 miles from a new development to a refining center at a public-utility return of 7 per cent is not, I submit, great. Perhaps at a higher return? If so, then this would be an economic cost of divorcement to the non-integrated refiners who are to be "helped" (and perhaps a cost to the majors as well). The non-integrated refiner would find himself paying more for transportation services from non-integrated lines than he did to the integrated company. (Remember that he already pays rates yielding 15 per cent, more or less, before taxes.) This writer cannot visualize several non-integrated pipe-line companies competing vigorously for a certificate of necessity[75] to build, say, a 24-inch, 300,000-barrel crude line from the Williston Basin (the new predicted bonanza) at some $100,000 per mile until that alleged bonanza has definitely proved itself; this it cannot do without the line. It was difficult enough to get integrated companies to build large-diameter lines from West Texas to the Gulf Coast;[76] yet any two more ideal terminals for crude trunk lines can hardly be imagined. Now it *is* possible that several companies might be willing to provide small lines, requiring lesser initial outlays, which would be constructed consecutively over a period of time as the field developed. This, however, is clearly an uneconomic operation. The economies of scale reported in the early part of this study show that duplication of small lines should be avoided. Any public policy which encourages it must be accepted only if there is nothing better. From this point we may turn to the implications for public policy which arise from the cost curves in Chapter I.

[74] "Entry," p. 901.

[75] "Entry," p. 896.

[76] Only in 1953 did West Texas get adequate capacity; see *World Oil*, October 1953, pp. 154–155.

IV

PUBLIC POLICY TOWARD CRUDE OIL PIPE LINES

It is possible to stipulate three general requisites of any public policy toward crude oil pipe lines:

(1) Acknowledging the existence of long-, intermediate-, and short-run decreasing costs in the operation of pipe lines, any acceptable public policy toward pipe lines must include provisions designed to achieve the social optimum of lowest cost per unit by encouraging the construction of the largest possible lines in any particular area. Because of the uneconomic higher costs (and therefore wasted resources) which arise from carrying oil in small quantities, any policy must be rejected if it encourages the construction of several small lines where one large line could be used.

(2) All companies desiring access to the lines should have the right thereto both initially and permanently guaranteed, in order that there can be no valid grounds for charges that the owners of the lines use them to control the producing and/or refining stages of the industry. Not only should there be guaranteed access, there should also be equalized costs for all companies using the lines.

(3) These two goals of any pipe-line public policy should be achieved with the least possible amount of regulatory effort. Indeed, should appreciable regulation be necessary, it would become necessary to balance the social desirability of least-cost operation and equal access against the undesirability of regulation.

Certain other requirements follow from the least-cost stipulation:

(1) All new fields should in general be served by only one crude oil trunk line, unless the MER of the field exceeds, say, 400,000 barrels per day; this line should be designed to carry the

capacity of the field, and its designed capacity operation should encompass the expected production of the field.

(2) On a strictly cost basis, it might even be wise not to utilize at a distance the output of small, isolated fields. Such crude would be relatively too expensive to move to connections with other, larger, trunk lines, or to refining centers. Such fields would be used only to serve immediately contiguous markets (with small, crude-oriented refineries).

(3) The single crude line would be laid to a terminal located in a geographically concentrated, market-oriented, or nodal point refining area, whence each refinery in the area could tap the trunk line with its own "gathering system." The terminal should be so located as to minimize the total cost of disbursing each refiner's expected crude requirements.

(4) Common stream crude usage for each type of crude shipped should be encouraged in order to minimize storage facilities, bookkeeping requirements, problems of contamination or intermingled crudes, and so forth.

A possible exception to the single-line system would be one where individually owned integrated lines from fields to refineries give such impressive economies of vertical integration (for one reason or another) that the losses in transportation costs incurred by using the small pipe lines would be more than offset by the economies of vertical integration. This exception is probably not an important one.

A more likely exception might be the case of a company having an isolated large crude-oriented refinery located where the crude source had been depleted, or where the local market had outgrown the local crude supply; such a company might well need to build its own small line in order to get sufficient crude. Similarly, two market-oriented refinery centers might be equally well located to use the crude from a given field. Two lines (each as large as feasible) would then be acceptable.

If industry performance is now lacking to a greater or lesser extent in meeting these goals, what kind of public policy can be designed to achieve them? Three solutions suggest themselves:

(1) independent common carriers, (2) integrated common carriers with common-carrier status rigidly enforced, or (3) joint ventures among majors, independents, and anyone else interested therein. The most appropriate device would seem to be the joint-venture system.

In the first place, a joint-venture policy would avoid the difficulties which the opponents of divorcement foresee in getting private capital sources outside the industry to invest substantial sums of money at 7 per cent in pipe-line transportation of crude oil. This problem becomes all-important when mass transportation is stipulated. How easy would it be to get non-integrated capital to invest in a risky 500- or 1000-mile, large-diameter line at, say, $100,000 per mile (initial outlay)? This problem has been discussed above; but it may be wise to summarize the argument once more, since the importance of this objection to new independent lines cannot be overemphasized.

The receiving, refinery terminal of a new line would be in a reasonably secure location if laid to a large refining center, since the oil companies have sufficient investments in well-located plants to preclude any great chance of shifts in the location of refineries. However, the other end of the crude trunk line is something else again, especially of crude trunk lines to new fields—those with which any public policy must be most concerned. Here such problems as unknown field capacity, unknown date of achieving substantial production (if ever), unknown length of time the field will produce, and others, would without doubt constitute serious barriers to the investment of non-integrated capital in major pipe lines. The anti-divestiture argument would assert with considerable force that outside capital would be most reluctant to invest under such conditions, that the possession of crude reserves in the field and/or of refining facilities to convert the crude into marketable products is a prerequisite to new pipeline construction into new fields. Rostow and Sachs both agree and disagree with this contention. This writer feels that the argument is especially important when applied to large-diameter lines.

Not only would a joint-venture system eliminate this problem, it also need not preclude those outside capital sources which might be interested in a flier in crude oil trunk lines from investing therein. The joint ventures could easily be combinations in one big pipe of independent common carriers serving independent refiners and integrated lines serving majors. Indeed, two such lines already exist (see the discussion following Table 2); these are the Canadian large-diameter systems from the new fields in Alberta to Ontario (Interprovincial) and to the Pacific Northwest (Trans-Mountain). These lines are jointly owned by majors, independent producers, independent refiners, large private interests, and the public. It is significant that the debt financing used in part to build them was underwritten by their major owners, who agreed to pay the interest on the bonds in the event that the lines could not do so.[1] In the Trans-Mountain case, for example, the six majors owning interests in the system underwrote the interest payments in proportion to their share of the *major* holdings in the line. In other words, if major company "A" held a 10 per cent share in a line, 50 per cent of which was owned by majors, then it would underwrite 20 per cent of the interest payments on the bonds. The advantages to outside capital sources are evident: they get lower-cost transportation for a given investment by joining with the large oil companies, and they get the advantage of the oil companies' credit position — without which the debt financing might well have not been forthcoming.

Second, divorcement would not be necessary under a system of joint ventures. Apart from the legal battles that would be avoided, any economies and other advantages of vertical integration that may exist, excluding those (if any) attributable to individual company ownership of pipe lines, would be preserved.

Third, a joint-venture system would remove the current practice, which is of doubtful constitutionality and economically unjust, that requires one company to provide transportation services with its money for any of its competitors who may desire such

[1] See the discussion of these companies in Moody's *Industrials.*

services. The Hepburn Act requires pipe lines to act as common carriers.[2] Consequently, when one oil company builds its own pipe line, it must, to conform with the law, build sufficient capacity to serve all others who might wish to use the line. This unjustifiable policy denying private-carrier privileges to the oil companies would be ended under a joint-venture system.

Fourth, access to the line would be guaranteed as a property right to those independents willing to buy a share; other independents not willing to buy a share could use any common-carrier facilities participating in the joint venture.

Finally, and most important, the use of joint ventures would permit the participating firms, large and small alike, to utilize to the greatest possible advantage the economies of scale characteristic of pipe-line operation — thereby giving every firm lower costs than it could achieve by operating its own line (since no firm has sufficient refinery capacity in any one area to build the most economic line on its own). The importance of this to the market-oriented independent refiner cannot be overemphasized. Take the case of a potential market-oriented independent refiner, located 1000 miles from his source of supply, who might wish to build a 30,000-barrel-per-day refinery. If he could get the necessary capital to build his own line (a 10-inch that requires an initial outlay of some $30 million), he would face a transportation cost of about 40 cents per barrel (4 per cent interest), compared with about 10 cents per barrel as one-tenth owner of a 30-inch, 300,000-barrel line. The initial outlay required for the large line would be only about $8.5 million, which could be had with the help of major-company credit ratings. Apart from the obvious advantage of having to obtain only 8.5 instead of 30 million dollars initially, how important is 30 cents per barrel to an independent refiner? Very important, since he might expect a spread of about one dollar per barrel between his crude price and aggregate revenue per barrel from the sale of refined products (assuming a market for residual fuel oil and no facilities for making lubricants). This margin has to cover transportation

[2] See fn. 3, page 76 above.

costs, refinery operating costs, selling costs, and other expenses — and provide a profit. Reducing the transportation costs from 40 per cent of the margin to 10 per cent might well be the difference between prosperity and bankruptcy. Thirty cents per barrel means $3.3 million per year for a 30,000-barrel refinery, compared with an initial investment of about $34 million ($8.5 million for the pipe line and $25.5 million for the refinery). If the company could break even with 40-cent transportation costs, it could return about 10 per cent on the investment with 10-cent transportation costs. Even if the refiner were located only 500 miles from the crude supply, there would be a saving of 15 cents per barrel.

A joint-venture system is, then, preferable to either independent common carriers, integrated lines with enforced common carrier status, or individually owned lines. Individually owned lines mean high costs. Enforced common-carrier lines deny private carrier privileges to oil companies and force one company to build capacity for its competitors. Large independent common carriers to new areas might well never be built; furthermore, provisions can be made for the inclusion of outside, common-carrier capital in joint ventures. However, many questions would be raised by the adoption of a policy designed to give a single-line, joint-venture pipe-line system. For example:

(1) To what extent is the industry achieving the public policy goals set out above, thereby making a positive public policy unnecessary?

(2) How could such a system be enforced? Or need it be enforced?

(3) Even if industry performance should be found lacking, is this a proper subject for public policy?

(4) To what extent should minimum transportation costs be sacrificed for national security reasons?

(5) To which refining area would the single line be laid?

(6) What is the capacity of the field which will determine the appropriate line size?

(7) How important a sacrifice of economies of vertical integration would be involved?

(8) Would not refiners desiring to enter the industry after a line is built be effectively barred under a joint-venture system, as opposed to a common-carrier system?

(9) Is there a conflict with the antitrust laws?

Each of these points will be discussed in turn.

(1) *Industry Performance.* Are the goals set up for a hypothetical public policy toward pipe lines being achieved to a greater or lesser extent by the industry without government interference? Perhaps it would be more accurate to describe these, not as goals for public policy, but as conditions which must obtain in this industry if (1) the social optimum of least cost transportation is to be achieved, and (2) entry into the refining stage of the industry is to be on its own merits and not subject to influence by oligopolistic pipe-line owners. If the industry is now achieving these goals substantially, then there would appear to be no reason for instituting any public policy.

To what extent have the trunk lines built in recent years satisfied these conditions? Insofar as the size of lines and throughputs is concerned, the trend in crude pipe-line construction since World War II has clearly been toward larger lines and larger crude throughputs in each line — a trend in the right economic direction, but one slow to start. Before World War II there were no large-diameter lines in the United States. The total mileage of crude trunk-line pipe over 12 inches in diameter in 1941 amounted to only 170 miles; in 1950 there were 4811 miles of such pipe,[3] and the total is now much higher. It was only after the construction of the "Big Inch" crude line from the Southwest to the East during the war that the use of large-diameter pipe began, even though it is inconceivable that the economies of scale characteristic of the operation of pipe lines were not widely known to the industry (since they derive from well-known physical relationships).

Indeed, there is abundant evidence (in the TNEC *Hearings*

[3] See A. T. Coombs and I. F. Avery, *Crude Oil and Refined Products Pipe Line Mileage in the United States,* United States Bureau of Mines Information Circular (Washington, 1950).

and the trade journals) that the economies of scale of large-volume transportation were well enough known before World War II. For example:

> For large-volume transportation the pipe line, the tanker, the barge, and more recently the transport truck, have all been developed to a high degree of efficiency. A very obvious point may perhaps be emphasized. Since many petroleum products . . . are in liquid form, increases in volume handled are accompanied by sharp reductions in unit transportation costs. Loading and unloading of large transportation units such as the 3,000,000 gallon tanker can be performed with relatively little personnel cost. Once loading is completed the difference in cost in moving a smaller and larger quantity is very small.[4]

Another witness quoted costs per barrel in large and small tankers for the Gulf Coast–East Coast run (11 cents versus 36 cents, with price increases before the large tankers were adopted).[5] At least as early as 1934, a pipe-line cost study appeared; this study points out the advantages of larger lines.[6] The paper showed that friction losses in large pipes are less than in small pipes and cited the costs of carrying 30,000 barrels per day in 8- and 10-inch lines (92 miles in length) as $0.06293 and $0.04577 per barrel, respectively.[7] Most significant, a 24-inch natural gas pipe line had been put in service by 1932.[8]

On the other hand, it was apparently not until 1942 that a technical article on crude oil pipe lines cited the advantages of lines as large as 24 inches.[9] This article points out that under conditions then existing, 10- or 12-inch lines were appropriate since the majority of new lines had capacities in the 25–50,000-

[4] Testimony of S. A. Swensrud (now president of Gulf) before the TNEC, *Hearings,* Part 15, p. 8675.

[5] Testimony of S. H. Pew (then chairman of Sun) before the TNEC, *Hearings,* Part 14, p. 7178.

[6] See F. R. Young, "Applied Design and Economics of Pipe Lines," *Oil and Gas Journal,* November 8, 1934, pp. 38 ff.

[7] Young, "Applied Design and Economics of Pipe Lines," p. 42.

[8] See the discussion of the Natural Gas Pipeline Company in *Standard and Poor.*

[9] E. G. Hill, "Engineering Economics of Long Petroleum Pipe Lines," American Institute of Mining and Metallurgical Engineers, *Transactions,* Petroleum Division, *Petroleum Development and Technology,* 1942, pp. 231 ff. See, especially, fig. 3, p. 234.

barrel range. The author therefore suggested that companies combine their transportation facilities, in which case lines of 20 to 24 inches would become economic.[10] Pipe sizes larger than 24 inches were ignored even at this date (chiefly because large welded pipe for lines over 26 inches did not become available until after World War II). The 1934 cost study ignores lines larger than 12 inches in diameter.[11] Even now there seems to be some aversion to admitting generally the advantages of very large lines. Articles still appear in the trade journals describing methods for sizing crude oil pipe lines. The most recent such article (September 1953) carries the problem only through 26-inch lines,[12] even though 32-inch pipe is being used for crude lines. The first quotation above from the TNEC proceedings cites the achievement of a "high degree of efficiency" in oil transportation, but the statement was made before any large-diameter lines had been built. Furthermore, in the TNEC hearings (and even later) industry personnel and commentators on transportation speak about "the" cost of carrying oil in pipe lines (especially when comparing costs of tanker, pipe line, and overland transportation). For example, in the TNEC *Hearings* a witness compares "the" costs of pipe-line transportation (3.2 mills per ton mile) and tanker transportation (1.25 mills per ton mile).[13] (The same testimony cites per cent of capacity operation and length of haul as the two "main variables" in pipe-line cost, with no reference to line diameter.)[14] Also, figures of the National Resources Planning Board (1942) are quoted in a recent transportation text as "the estimated average costs of transportation of petroleum." [15]

[10] Hill, "Engineering Economics of Long Petroleum Pipe Lines," p. 238.

[11] F. R. Young, "Applied Design," *Oil and Gas Journal*, November 8, 1934, p. 41.

[12] W. L. Kennedy, Jr. and Charles G. Stueve, "Sizing Crude Oil Pipe Lines," *Oil and Gas Journal*, September 21, 1953, pp. 183 ff. This article updates cost data originally prepared by G. G. Hughes in a thesis at the University of Texas. See G. G. Hughes, The Preliminary Design of Crude Oil Trunk Systems (Austin, 1949), unpublished thesis deposited in the Library of the University of Texas.

[13] Testimony of F. B. Dow, TNEC *Hearings*, Part 15, p. 8591. Cites J. E. Pogue, *Economics of the Petroleum Industry*, March 1939.

[14] Dow, TNEC *Hearings*, p. 8592.

[15] See M. L. Fair and E. W. Williams, Jr., *Economics of Transportation* (New York, 1950), p. 106.

Speaking of *the* cost of carrying oil in pipe lines (or tankers) is nonsense, since costs per barrel-mile vary with the size of line (or tanker) used and the amount of oil transported. Even averages of per barrel costs have little meaning when the per barrel cost can range from 8 to 50 cents per barrel per thousand miles.

Consequently, it must be concluded that even though ignorance was not a factor in the slowness of the industry in adopting large lines, there is some evidence that engineering and managerial personnel have been reluctant to admit the known facts — especially in the case of very large lines, say those over 24 inches. It is impossible to determine the extent to which this reluctance has affected the development of economic transportation. However, it is safe to say that managerial and engineering conservatism has produced some hesitancy in moving to new, untried, revolutionary line sizes and has, therefore, been a factor in retarding the development of economic lines.

A more important reason for the backwardness in adopting economic pipe-line transportation has probably been a reluctance to make the necessary large expenditures. Since the capacity of a new field cannot be determined precisely, crude pipe lines are, as has been pointed out above, hazardous investments. It is not unnatural for company managements to hesitate to spend the very large sums required for large, economic pipe lines before they are certain that large lines will be needed. Furthermore, to the extent that the lines are not financed from plowed-back profits, it is also necessary to convince the financial community of the desirability of spending $75,000 to $100,000 per mile for pipe lines 500 to 1000 miles long.

Another explanation has been that some of the large companies have been reluctant to participate in joint ventures when they were being subjected to criticism for alleged monopolistic control of the industry. Those participating in crude joint ventures were specifically criticized in the TNEC *Monograph* on the oil industry:

In order to lessen competition and to make their crude oil transportation more profitable, 8 of the 20 major companies have combined with one or more other majors to build and use the facilities on a common basis. No independent has any interest in these lines.[16]

Combining in an economic pipe line, then, has invited criticism for suppressing competition. Of course, no one company can even now build economic lines unless they are to be used by others. This was even more the case in the 1930's, when all companies were smaller.

Indeed, the most important reason for the lack of economic lines before World War II was without doubt that the industry was not big enough as a whole. Total production in Texas, the largest producing state, was only 510,000 barrels per day in 1937, the peak prewar year.[17] A considerable part of this was on the Gulf Coast, where large trunk lines are not needed. Only 309,000 barrels per day were produced in West Texas, the most important originating source of pipe-line crude.[18] This was sufficient capacity for only one economic line, and for that only if the oil were sent to one destination. It was not until 1944 that production in West Texas surpassed 380,000 barrels per day — the capacity of one of the lines serving that area today. By 1952 production in West Texas was 1,240,000 barrels per day — enough for several lines. In other words, an external, industry-wide economy of scale has developed permitting the use of economic lines. Even so, there still has seemed to be some reluctance on the part of company managements to move immediately toward giant lines, probably because of the large initial outlays required. As was noted above, it was only in 1953 that sufficient capacity was provided for West Texas; and some of this has been small-diameter capacity.

The trend in crude pipe-line construction since World War II is shown in Table 2 above. This table includes most of the major projects built since 1946, covering a total throughput capacity of 3.3 million barrels per day, out of a total system capacity of something over four million barrels per day. It will be observed

[16] R. C. Cook, TNEC *Monograph* No. 39, *Control of the Petroleum Industry by Major Oil Companies* (Washington, 1941), p. 26.

[17] See *World Oil,* February 15, 1953, p. 190.

[18] See *World Oil,* October 1953, p. 130, for these and the following production data.

that there are only a few lines having diameters smaller than 18 inches. Furthermore, both diameters and throughputs have been increasing year by year as the industry has grown and as the cultural lag, so to speak, in the minds of oil company executives against introducing revolutionary transportation facilities and spending tremendous sums of money initially for pipe lines has begun to disappear. The fact that there is a trend toward large lines does not necessarily mean that the trend has gone far enough even now. The largest line yet built in the United States for crude is 26 inches. This 26-inch line has a capacity of 381,000 barrels per day, while the optimum for this throughput according to the cost curves in Chapter I would be a 30- or 32-inch line. Line sizes in general seem to be somewhat less than would be indicated by the cost curves. However, it is probably safe to assume that the industry would move to 30-inch or larger pipe in the future if there were a new field which justified such a line. The Trans-Arabian pipe line is 30 and 31 inches in diameter; this line moves crude from the geographically concentrated, prolific field in Arabia (a field held by only a few owners) to water transportation on the Mediterranean. The Iraq petroleum company line moving crude from Iraq to the Mediterranean is 26, 30, and 32 inches (a smaller line was originally planned and then abandoned). These lines were built in concert by the small number of companies owning interests in the Middle East producing areas. The Canadian extension of Interprovincial is also a 30-inch line.

Should new prolific fields be developed in the United States, similar lines would be expected. However, crude ownership in the United States is spread among more major companies and many independents. As a result, it is more difficult to organize joint-venture lines encompassing all owners; consequently there may be a danger of building, say, two small parallel lines where one large line would have sufficed.

Some small trunk lines are still being built in addition to gathering lines which are necessarily small. Many of these are what might be called "intra-regional" trunk lines. A company planning a crude-oriented refinery might well be expected to locate near any large urban center in that area, using gathering lines for crude supplies immediately contiguous to the city. However, it might also own crude supplies in the same general area, but perhaps one or two hundred miles away. Under these conditions it might build an "intra-regional" small-diameter line to tap its own crude sources. Hence the lines built by Phillips and Continental from West Texas to Oklahoma (see Table 2). If the field is served by a large trunk line moving crude to a major refining center, a small, intra-regional line is possibly uneconomic (if some accessible point on the large line is closer to the field than the refinery in question). It is interesting to note that this uneconomic movement of crude, to the extent that it is uneconomic, may well be attributable in part to the fact that the company is too *small,* and in part to the fact that it is vertically integrated. If the company in question had sufficient reserves near the urban center, it would not have needed to build the small line. If it had no reserves of its own, then it would have had no reason for using distant supplies if others were available. On the other hand, there might not have been sufficient crude near the refinery, either due to growth of the local market or a decline in the local producing capacity. In this case, the intra-regional small line would be justified.

It may be concluded that small crude trunk lines, while once the only type used, are becoming less and less important. Line sizes may not have advanced quite so rapidly as was possible; but this is hardly a sufficient reason for government intervention, since it would be an optimist indeed who would predict that government regulation would be precise enough to give us 30-inch lines instead of 26-inch lines. An important problem may be that of laying two small lines where one very large one could have been used. This is attributable to widespread ownership of crude, and perhaps to the reluctance of some companies to enter into joint ventures. This might be an appropriate field for public action.

A problem related to that of laying parallel lines is outright overbuilding — laying lines to more than one destination such that there is excess pipe-line capacity and, hence, high-cost transportation. Duplication of facilities out of West Texas was quite possibly avoided in 1951 (after a prior shortage of facilities) only by government action through the mechanism of PAD steel allocations. The PAD found that four large pipe lines were proposed out of West Texas, two to the Pacific Coast, two to the Gulf Coast (one direct, the other via East Texas where it connects with a system to Ohio). Building all of these lines would have meant excess pipe-line capacity in relation to the area MER (and hence unnecessary steel use). For these reasons the PAD was forced to choose, and chose the two lines to the Gulf Coast which aggregate about 600,000 barrels per day in capacity (about a third of this replaces small lines).[19] In the absence of such government action, equivalent almost to the granting of public utility certificates of necessity, it is possible that a non-regulated industry would have overbuilt. However, the PAD seems subsequently to have receded from its original position, since one independent West Texas–West Coast large-diameter line was approved late in 1952, once the steel shortage began to ease. Perhaps Rostow and Sachs were not so wrong after all in their contentions that integrated companies build too fast and too slow. Perhaps the industry as now organized does, paradoxically, both underbuild and overbuild. This situation is not, however, due to vertical integration. Rather, it is the result of the presence of a number of competing firms in the industry. Underbuilding at first and overbuilding later (in response to the proving of the field) is a cumulative reaction analogous to the "error" theory of the business cycle which asserts that many competing firms expand to meet the needs of new markets — so many that too much new capacity is created.[20] The excess capacity is a cost of competition. In the case of new oil fields there is a reluctance to build pipe lines at first; if a bonanza then develops, there is a rush which may, if unsupervised, give too much capacity. This might well

[19] See PAD, *Transportation of Oil,* p. 34.

[20] See G. Haberler, *Prosperity and Depression,* 3rd ed., United Nations publication (Lake Success, New York, 1946), pp. 111–112.

be a case where some government coördination, if not regulation, would actually be to the advantage of the companies involved.

So much for industry performance in regard to sizes of lines and throughputs. Are independents getting access to the new, large lines? This subject has been discussed above insofar as past common carrier access is concerned, with the conclusion that the evidence on physical access is too meager for any valid conclusions. Insofar as rates are concerned, it was found that there has been a modest decrease (10 per cent) since the beginning of serious rate regulation in 1941. However, as has been repeatedly asserted in this study, there is without doubt little use of crude trunk lines by independent refiners simply because there is not very much independent refining capacity so located that it needs the trunk lines. A much more important question is the matter of physical access to the new, efficient pipe-line systems.

Whether the integrated lines will grant common-carrier privileges to those independents (if any) who want them remains to be seen for the new systems which are just beginning operation. Most of the new lines have excess capacity during the current depressed period (1954) in domestic crude production; under these conditions, the lines are doubtless glad to get any outside common-carrier business offered. However this question may be answered once the lines begin to operate at capacity, there is a recent (non-regulated) development which will guarantee to participating independent refiners the physical access to crude supplies which they desire. This is the extension of crude pipe-line joint ventures to include smaller, formerly non-integrated refiners as well as majors. The most important example of such a joint venture in the United States is the Rancho system discussed in Chapters II and III, which is a joint venture among four majors and three large independents which have refineries around Houston. The benefits which accrue to well-located independent refiners — lower initial outlays than for singly owned lines, much lower total transportation costs than in singly owned lines, guaranteed access to crude, and so forth — were discussed at the beginning of this chapter. This particular system does, indeed, conform closely to the "ideal" set up in the goals for public policy. Each independent gets physical access guaranteed as a property right to crude supplies; and he gets his transportation by paying for it, not by using lines built and maintained by his competitors under legal compulsion which requires that they offer him pipe-line service for public-utility returns.

A similar development, which is even closer to the best that any public policy could hope to achieve, is illustrated by the two Canadian lines mentioned above which were built under special permits from the Canadian Government. In these lines some independent refiners have paid for a share initially; others can use the portions of the line owned by outside interests, thereby foregoing an initial outlay but later paying a rate sufficient to compensate the independent owners of the line for the use of their funds and for the risk taken. In the Trans-Mountain line there are even independent producers who have ownership shares. If future crude lines built in the United States were to imitate those built in Canada (most of the ownership is by United States companies or their subsidiaries), then there would be little ground for complaint about major exclusion of the market-oriented independent refiners from crude supplies.

The question, of course, is whether all large oil companies will be so impressed by the cost savings to be had from mass transportation in lines larger than any company can use alone that they will in the future voluntarily permit, or encourage, independent refiners also to take advantage of the lower costs in order that their (the large companies') costs may be even further lowered. It is clear that the majors need each other for cost savings in joint ventures much more than they need any new independents, since the additional volume any such new independent could provide would be relatively small. For example, adding an independent with a capacity of 50,000 barrels per day to a 250,000-barrel-per-day joint venture planned by majors would cut the cost less than one cent per barrel per 1000 miles — a small cost saving if there were other factors weighing against the admittance of the independent.

Whether independents would be admitted voluntarily depends on a chain of circumstances: (1) whether the majors have actually had an exclusionary, monopolistic intent in controlling the pipe lines; (2) whether the majors feel that they can maintain their positions by competitive advantages arising from economies of vertical integration, if any; (3) whether the majors believe that independent refiners operating small plants on purchased crude can compete cost-wise with large refineries operated to a large extent by their own crude; (4) whether the majors believe that any new independents who might be able to engage in effective competition will do so, for example, by starting price wars, or will live and let live in the best oligopolistically rational fashion; (5) whether the majors feel that their position in the refined products market can be maintained by existing good will, advertising, financial strength, and so forth, in the face of new entry if the new entrants should not live and let live — in short, whether the majors *themselves* feel that the stability of the market for refined products and their dominant position in the industry are dependent on an oligopsonist-oligopolist squeeze (actual or potential) achieved through pipe-line ownership. If they should believe any of this, then they might well be willing to sacrifice a small lowering of transportation costs to prevent new entry into refining.

The majors might also be deterred from such joint ventures by fear of government antitrust prosecution for combining with their fellow majors in an economic adventure; this point will be discussed presently.

The reader will without doubt do his own speculating on whether the major companies will or will not accept independents into future joint ventures. This writer tends to feel that they will if there are fairly large amounts of crude involved; for small tenders, say, 5000 barrels per day, there might be some reluctance. The cost saving is negligible, and there might well be that much excess capacity in the line from day to day if it were large without the independents; under these conditions the majors could even satisfy the Hepburn Act. (It should be noted that unless the new independents were considerably larger than five or ten thousand barrels per day, they could do little or nothing to influence the price of refined products.) That the following companies (or their affiliates) have to date participated in joint ventures including one or more independents (although only five such ventures exist in crude lines) may be some indication of the future attitude of the majors: Standard (New Jersey), Standard (Indiana), Shell, Socony, Sinclair, Standard (California), Texas Company, Gulf, Sun, Pure, Continental, Phillips, and the Ohio Oil Company.[21] (Union originally participated in Trans-Mountain, but later sold its share.) Neither Jersey nor Royal Dutch-Shell nor any of the other majors has ever been seriously accused of not being able to take care of its own interests.

It may be said, then, that the industry is building larger lines and carrying larger conglomerate amounts of crude oil at lower costs, without benefit of government assistance. However, duplication of facilities is still a problem; the laying of small lines is a lesser problem. Government action was used in 1951 to prevent the building of alleged duplicate facilities out of the most important single area acting as a source for crude trunk-line shipments. There is a real economic incentive (cheaper transportation) for the majors to grant the independents a share in new lines, although the lowering of cost is not appreciable unless a rather large amount of new independent capacity is involved. Whether this incentive will be accepted on a wide scale in the future depends on several factors, but principally on (1) how important the majors themselves consider their control of pipe lines to be in maintaining their positions in the industry, and (2) how much volume the independents can provide. All eight of the giant companies and six of the other eleven majors have participated in four crude trunk-line joint ventures including independents of one sort or another.

(2) *Enforcement*. The solution proposed here for enforcement

[21] See Table 2 (General Notes). Richfield owns a share of Trans-Mountain; therefore, Cities Service might also be included since Cities Service and Sinclair control Richfield.

of a system of single-line joint ventures is the requirement of a government permit as a prerequisite to the construction of a crude trunk line (trunk lines would be defined as those, say, 100 miles in length and over). Such permits would be granted only if certain conditions were fulfilled:

(a) That all companies or outside private interests desiring shares of the line be granted an interest therein — if they could demonstrate both the ability to pay their share of the initial outlay and subsequent operating costs and the likelihood of their being able to use the share sought. The share must be used to avoid subsequent operating costs that would of necessity be higher than if the share were not granted. (Remember that short-run costs per barrel-mile are higher than intermediate-run costs — see Chapter I). If extra stations are added to a planned line to take care of a new participant who does not use the line, then the other companies would incur the extra initial and subsequent operating costs of the extra capacity — costs which would not have been incurred if this capacity had not been added. As a result, the original participants would have higher costs than necessary.

(b) That the line must be of a size that will carry economically the MER capacity of the field which can be expected in the immediate future, as determined from estimates of the participating companies and the relevant government agency, with provision for future expansion by the addition of more stations.

(c) That duplication of facilities must be discouraged, especially where the duplication takes the form of small parallel lines.

(d) That each company will have property rights enforceable by civil suit to a share of the line proportionate to its share of the original investment costs. In other words, the joint-venture line would simply be a combination in one pipe of as many small lines as there are interested companies, with operation by one company for purposes of efficiency, but with contractual and property-ownership protection for the other participants against any temptation the operator might have to exclude them from their share.

These permits would be similar to traditional public utility certificates of convenience and necessity. There would, however, be at least one major difference. In general, as will be seen in the subsequent discussion, the regulatory body would not have the power to deny any bona fide applicants the right to build capacity (as members of a joint venture). Its function would be to promote the building of economic capacity and to promote equal access to lines for all willing to pay for it — not to determine (as does the Federal Power Commission for gas lines) the maximum capacity that should be built. In other words, these permits would not be used to protect one selected group against the competition of others.

There are, as is probably inevitable with proposals for government regulation of any sort, certain objections which immediately arise to an equal-access permit system. Most of these are the objections to the joint-venture system which were listed above (see page 133) and which will be discussed later. There is, however, one objection to the permit per se. This is that pipe-line permit decisions would without doubt have to be subject to appeal to the courts. Why should this cause misgivings? For the answer the reader need only look to the fiasco which arose over piping of natural gas to New England.[22] Natural gas pipe lines can only be built after a certificate of necessity and convenience is granted by the Federal Power Commission. Two companies, Algonquin (a subsidiary of Texas Eastern) and Northeastern (a subsidiary of Tennessee), applied for the right to serve New England. The Commission granted certificates dividing the market in a manner favoring Texas Eastern which then built its line; but about the time the line was scheduled to go into service, Texas Eastern was presented with a court injunction forbidding delivery until the courts could review the case. The losers had appealed and gained a no-delivery order. Subsequently, the dispute was "compromised" practically as originally decided by the FPC, but for months in the meantime New England had no natural gas and Texas Eastern had a useless pipe line. Should such a situation

[22] See *Gas Age,* August 27, 1953, pp. 48 ff.

occur in crude oil pipe lines, it could well mean that the time required for the construction of new lines for new fields might be as long as or longer than the foes of dissolution assert would be the case if only non-integrated lines were permitted (these would also probably have to have permits). This delay might in turn create barriers to exploration and field development.

Is such a situation likely in the case of crude oil pipe lines? A case can be hypothesized where purely nuisance interference might occur. Assume that oil company X has a large refinery in a large refinery area; the refinery is supplied from the company's principal holdings in a field 1000 miles away. Then a new field is discovered only 400 miles from this refining area, but company X does not participate in the rush for leases in this new field. It would be quite likely to do all in its power to prevent the construction of a pipe line which could deliver at 40 per cent of the transportation cost it incurs by bringing its crude from 1000 miles away. If an equal-access permit were required as a prerequisite to line construction, then X could demand a large share in the line. This would be refused both by the participating companies and the agency unless X could establish the existence of independent crude in the field which it expected to tap at the market price instead of using its own more distant crude at cost. If X were granted the right of appeal to the courts, it could delay for months or years the utilization of the field. Such a case is probably unimportant simply because most companies own reserves in all areas and are forced to follow the oil play into any new area in order to maintain their positions; but it might be a danger.

A possible device to minimize the danger of such nuisance interference is an apportionment of costs in such a way as to penalize companies which do not utilize their shares of the line. All companies would, under this plan, pay the per-barrel cost of shipping at the full capacity of the line on all oil shipped. If the line operated at less than capacity, then this payment would not meet the total costs (since there are decreasing short-run costs). The difference between actual cost and what the minimum cost would have been had the excess capacity not been built would be paid by those companies operating at less than capacity; the apportionment would be in proportion to the amount of unused capacity of each company. For example, assume that capacity per-barrel cost payments left a line with a loss of $100,000 in a given month and that two companies were responsible, one shipping at a rate 10,000 barrels below its capacity, the other shipping at a rate 20,000 barrels below its capacity. Also assume that if the excess 30,000 barrels had not been provided for, the minimum cost per month would have been $10,000 per month higher (costs per barrel *must* rise for smaller throughputs).[23] The $90,000($100,000 — $10,000) would be split one to two. The company shipping 10,000 barrels less than its capacity caused one-third of the excess cost; it would pay $30,000. The company shipping 20,000 barrels less than its capacity caused two-thirds of the excess costs; it would pay $60,000. The other $10,000 would be allocated among the other owners, since they would have had to pay more per barrel if the extra capacity had not been built. Practically, of course, longer periods might be used; and it would probably be simpler to begin with the cost at, say, 95 per cent of capacity, since for reasons of logistics no company would be likely to ship at 100 per cent of capacity all of the time. In addition, exceptions to the penalty rule would probably have to be made for bona fide shipments at less than capacity, for example, when a refinery is shut down for repairs.

Under such a penalty provision any company which applied for admission could be accepted without question since it could be accepted without financial danger to the other participants. If it failed to use its share of the line, it alone would pay the resulting extra costs per barrel. Nuisance interference would be quite expensive, since any company planning such interference would have to be prepared to pay for the capacity requested — regardless of whether the capacity were used. Some such penalty provi-

[23] Unless this excess were an addition to the line made subsequent to its construction, in which case the offenders would simply be charged the extra costs over the original costs.

sions should make nuisance troubles of this sort negligible and thereby minimize the necessity of court appeal.

Nuisance interference, then, can be dealt with by making it expensive. Furthermore, it is not likely that there would be much cause for appeal to the courts if a regulatory body persuaded two groups of applicants for parallel small lines to coalesce; this again appeals to the pocketbook by saving transportation costs for all concerned. Indeed, if managements are rational and the major oil companies themselves believe their repeated assertions that they do not own pipe lines to control the rest of the industry, then there should be no need for enforcement in this situation. However, if there were two groups really competing for the dubious honor of building a large-diameter line out of a new field, as the two gas companies were competing for a new market, then there could be real dangers of delay. Such a situation might arise if two groups desired to build lines equal to the expected field capacity to different refining areas. Here court appeal of the regulatory body's decision would be almost a certainty, and court appeal would even more certainly mean delay in providing the service. Further misgivings arise. Is this the kind of decision government has a right to make in a free-enterprise economy? Because of its importance, should it arise again, as it did in the PAD decision discussed above, this case will be discussed at some length in connection with the third, fourth, and fifth objections to joint ventures (see page 133).

(3) *Appropriateness of Public Policy in This Field.* It is now necessary to ask whether pipe-line regulation of the sort discussed here is in reality a proper area for government regulation under any conditions. One of the most important reasons for instituting such a program would be the avoidance of parallel inefficient facilities. A lesser reason might be to avoid outright overbuilding. There is a fairly clear case for coördination that would result in the combining of planned parallel small lines into one big line; not only would the social optimum of least-cost transportation result, there would also be lower costs for all companies concerned. Probably few objections would be raised to this type

of activity by a government agency. Indeed, should the management of one company refuse to participate in a joint venture in favor of building its own line, it would, everything else being equal, be doing its stockholders a real dis-service. Any management which turned down transportation costs of 10 cents per barrel for 40 cents per barrel would be behaving with impressive economic irrationality, unless there were other reasons for refusing to participate.

On the other hand, is the prevention of overbuilding of capacity by the use of certificates of necessity and convenience a valid function of government in a free-enterprise economy? In times of national emergency it is, but in normal times there are serious questions about such regulation. This is in large part a political matter, but there are also economic considerations. It is, on the surface, uneconomic to build twice as much pipe-line capacity as is needed from a field. But is it necessarily uneconomic? Suppose a regulatory agency chose one of two proposed terminals and forbade the other. Would this be an economically defensible action if there were a population shift from the chosen area, or if closer crude supplies were found a year or so later? Should either of these happen, the action of the regulatory agency would, in the end, be unwise. For this reason the agency should probably not be given the power of choosing terminals. If two groups desire to build lines from a field to different refining areas, then both groups should be permitted to do so (with competition the final determinant of which line is to be most used) except perhaps in cases of momentous national importance, cases which are unlikely to occur very frequently.

Even if the regulatory body made decisions which proved in the end to be economically wise, there would still be serious political objections to a policy which permits government to decide whether new capacity may be built in any industry in a free-enterprise economy. This amounts to political usurpation of the private right to make investment decisions. Even if granted in the name of economic efficiency, such a power should be given to government only after a careful comparison of the disadvantages of potential waste from overbuilding by competitive firms with the disadvantages to an economy of government regulation of the amount of capacity in an industry. Such regulation exists, of course, in the United States in the public-utility field. Crude oil pipe lines, as a system of transportation, could be brought under similar restraints with no particular danger of establishing precedents for other industries outside the public-utility field. However, this writer would be content to limit the power of the permit-granting agency to combination of individual lines from a field to any given terminal and to omit from its jurisdiction the power to deny any group the right to build a line, at least in normal times.

In addition to the economic and political objections to limiting pipe-line capacity from a field, there is yet another reason for questioning the right of government to apply a public policy of joint ventures to the pipe-line problem. Has government the right to insist that oil company X participate in a joint venture if X prefers, for one reason or another, to build its own pipe line? Put another way, has government the right to deny oil company X the right to build its own pipe line for its own use, costly though it might be to the company? Granted that it would be uneconomic for X to refuse to participate in a large-diameter pipe line, is it a proper function of government to make a private enterprise behave efficiently if the enterprise chooses not to? In this case the question is even more complex because refusal of one company to participate means higher transportation costs for *all* companies because of the economies of scale. Can government force one company to behave efficiently if it does not choose to do so in order to permit the whole industry to operate more efficiently and thereby achieve the socially desirable conditions of minimum costs for the industry as a whole?

If the reader would prefer not to have to answer this question, he may find comfort in the rationalization that in a competitive industry the problem is not very likely to occur. If one company refuses to accept transportation costs which are considerably lower than those accepted by its competitors, the individualist will find himself at a competitive disadvantage. Indeed, one might ask why any company would decline to participate. There are legal problems involved in working out the details of joint ventures, be the ventures government-inspired or otherwise. These the writer will not attempt to discuss; however, it would seem likely that the legal technicalities can be solved. There is another possible reason for avoiding joint ventures, a reason which has undoubtedly caused some oil companies to avoid them. This is the danger of adverse publicity, if not of legal action, resulting from participation by the major oil companies in joint ventures which have been labeled as monopolistic devices designed to disguise a conspiracy to control the industry.

To summarize: in a free economy, government regulation should be limited to the combination of any parallel lines planned from a given field to a given refinery terminal. Government should not in general have the power to choose terminals, should there be applications to build to more than one. Furthermore, government may not have the right to deny any firm permission to build its own pipe line, uneconomic though it may be; this is not, however, likely to be a serious problem in competitive industries. Three qualifications were raised to these propositions: (a) the question of normal times, (b) the possibility of terminal decisions involving questions of momentous national importance, and (c) the question of the accusation of monopoly. Each of these will be discussed in some detail in sections 4, 5, and 9 respectively.

(4) *National Security.* There are important questions of national security involved. Economists would probably prefer to discuss problems in the realm of normal periods. However, we are now forced to face the fact that abnormality has become normal, that national security questions cannot be ignored in an industry such as the oil industry which provides a scarce resource of great military importance that is in limited supply. Because of this, it might conceivably be necessary to sacrifice some pipeline economies. Perhaps the geographical concentration of refining that would be promoted by any conscious (or non-regulated)

program of large crude lines is militarily unwise. Similarly, perhaps it is necessary to tap small isolated fields, otherwise uneconomic, for distant use in order to have access to all reserves. The choice of refining center as a terminal must also consider military supply factors, even if geographic dispersion is not deemed essential. All of these questions would have to be considered by a regulatory agency. On the other hand, the agency should consider the problem of wasted steel from duplicate facilities from a security viewpoint. Note that encouraging one large line minimizes *both* steel usage and costs per barrel relative to steel usage and costs in several parallel lines (assuming correct wall-thickness practices). Not only is steel conserved by preventing overbuilding of pipe-line capacity, it is also conserved by substituting one line for several parallel lines since more barrels per day per ton of steel can be had in large than in small lines.[24]

Consequently, it may be said that security problems may justify government regulation of private investment decisions in planning new pipe-line capacity — regulation that would otherwise be politically unacceptable. It is even possible that military considerations might necessitate some government regulation which necessitates a sacrifice of cost savings. These are, however, problems that are not connected with the problem of pipeline control by the major oil companies. If and when they arise, they will have to be solved either under the present regulatory system or any other regulatory system. For this reason they should not affect public policies designed to prevent monopoly.

(5) *Choice of Terminal.* Should more than one terminal be desired for pipe-line transport from a particular field, the case hypothesized in section (2) above, what would a regulatory agency do if the case is really important? If the regulatory body is given the power to choose, its decisions will be crucial, because once made, there will be a substantial buried capital investment

[24] In times of war it might, of course, be deemed desirable to use small lines (thereby substituting steel for power and labor) if steel were less scarce than other factors of production used in pipe-line transportation.

which without doubt will be used so long as the field can be produced economically. The locational effects on refining, however irrational, which would arise from such a choice would be permanent. Since the choice is so permanent in its consequences, some discretion should be allowed to any regulatory body. If the problem involves proposals for, say, two 200,000-barrel lines to separate refining centers out of a 400,000-barrel field, then a regulatory body should approve both. Some advantage would be taken of pipe-line economies of scale, even though somewhat cheaper transportation could have been had with a line to only one center. (Note that two *parallel* 200,000-barrel lines should never be constructed concurrently.)

However, the problem faced by the PAD in choosing between the Gulf and Pacific Coast terminals from West Texas[25] might conceivably arise again. It is in the case where there are proposals for two 200,000-barrel lines to different refining centers from a *200,000*-barrel field that the problem may become serious. If the regulatory body is to decide between proposals, the closer center might be chosen. However, that center might have sufficient crude from other sources to satisfy its existing refineries. If the (industry) demand curve for gasoline is relatively horizontal, then more crude into that market might be helpful in encouraging independent refineries; if the demand curve is relatively vertical, then the extra crude would be relatively useless. In general, as was pointed out in section (2) above, the agency should approve both applications and let the forces of competition decide which would be used.

There has recently been a basic dispute (of which the West Texas problem already mentioned was a part) in the industry which illustrates the possible extent of the problem. The question was how to relieve the oil shortage in California, where crude production capacity was thought to be insufficient to serve future Pacific Coast needs.[26] Importing to California from overseas was

[25] See page 69.

[26] The matter was debated publicly at the allowable hearing of the Texas Railroad Commission on February 18, 1953, even though official decisions had been reached in 1950.

then felt to be an uneconomic operation. Two other solutions were offered. One was to bring crude from West Texas to Los Angeles. The other (favored by most large companies) was to bring Alberta crude to the Pacific Northwest, where it would be used to start a new refining center capable of serving that area. This would leave California oil for the Californians and would, so it was predicted, balance supply and consumption there. The proponents of Texas-to-California shipments asserted that Eastern Canada could use the Alberta crude, why bring it into the United States? To which the other side replied that they preferred to make up any deficiency that might occur in Eastern Canada by moving Texas crude to the Gulf, thence to the sea to Maine, and thence to the Montreal refineries by pipe line (or possibly by tanker all the way). (The problem might also be solved by using Venezuelan or Arabian crude, a point soft-pedaled because of the political implications.) The result of this was the PAD decision noted above to approve the Trans-Mountain pipe line from Alberta to Vancouver and Washington and the two lines from West Texas to the Gulf Coast. A moment's reflection will indicate the momentous importance of this decision. It has committed the industry to two major pipe-line systems out of Alberta (one west, the other east to Ontario), to the creation of refining capacity in Washington, to the continued use of tanker shipments from the Gulf or overseas for the Montreal refineries, to the use of California crude in California refineries to serve only the California market, and so forth. These decisions are permanent and their effect will be with us for the foreseeable future.[27] However, how often will such a decision as West Texas versus Canada have to be made? This momentous case is certainly atypical. Furthermore, court appeal of any decision would be permitted under the system advocated here so that full publicity and judicial review before the regulatory agency would be available to the party losing the case. Appeals would doubtless occur in cases such as this. In this

[27] In spite of the original PAD decision, one of the groups which planned to ship crude from Texas to California as an independent common carrier subsequently announced its intention of building the line (steel was by then readily available); as of late 1954, however, construction had not been started.

rare case, the delay might well, in this writer's opinion, be worth its cost. It is probably unwise for such decisions to be made by a regulatory agency on its own. Here, in the only case where court appeal would be likely, the appeal would be desirable (especially if purely legal delay could be minimized) in order to give the case the careful consideration it deserves.

Leaving such decisions in the hands of a government agency (especially where there was no appeal, as in the PAD case) is, it must be repeated, a far departure from free enterprise. The only justifications are those already pointed out: (1) national security, (2) economic waste, and (3) the fact that such momentous decisions as this one would occur very rarely.

(6) *The Problem of Field Capacity.* If it should be decided that the industry's performance leaves something to be desired and that a positive public policy should be instituted, an unavoidable task to be taken up by those responsible for the policy would be a decision on how large a given line should be. As large as the capacity of the field. But how large will the field capacity be? One never knows precisely what the capacity of any oil field will be until all of its oil has been used up; however, it is apparent that a bonanza field in a nonpopulated area will never be used up if it has no transportation facilities. Therefore, if the planning body were to wait until the field capacity had been definitely established, it would have to wait indefinitely. The regulatory agency must make some estimate of a quantity which is in reality unknown at the time the estimate must be made. In a new area a 30-inch line might be needed, perhaps several 30-inch lines. On the other hand, the same new area which showed bright promise at first might turn out to be large enough only for local refineries, and hence might not justify the construction of a trunk line at all.

A partial solution to this problem in current industry practice is the building of a fairly large line, say 24 inches, after a period of some time, but a line with few stations. Subsequent field capacity increases, if any, can be met by the addition of new stations. The ultimate capacity would be carried at a higher cost than if a

30-inch line had been built originally, but not necessarily at a higher cost per barrel than the initial throughput, since the large-diameter intermediate run curves are relatively flat for rather wide ranges of output. Indeed, costs per barrel might be down somewhat below their original level.[28] Should the new capacity not develop, then other capacity need not be carried at higher costs than necessary because of the operation of a 30-inch line at less than capacity. In any event, the regulatory body entrusted with pipe-line public policy decisions would be faced with this problem, which in the last analysis has no answer. The best effort is an intelligent guess, based perhaps on the capacities of lines suggested by various interested pipe-line companies, crude producers, or refiners.

(7) *Economies of Vertical Integration.* It is possible that individually owned trunk lines from fields to individual refineries would give such impressive economies of vertical integration (for one reason or another) that the losses in transportation costs incurred by using small pipe lines instead of joint ventures would be more than offset by the economies of vertical integration? As far as actual published evidence on economies of vertical integration is concerned, Professor Bain finds that the effect of vertical integration on costs is approximately neutral.[29] Professor Rostow does not find cause to dispute this. Even if there are important economies of vertical integration, the fact that there are joint-venture crude and products lines serving several refineries in a given area seems to indicate that any such economies present in the petroleum industry are not drastically reduced by multi-company ownership of pipe lines. On the other hand, some companies have more or less balanced systems,[30] whether by preference or force of circumstance it is hard to say. It would seem, however, that any economies of vertical integration which might exist from not having to plan for interruption in the crude supply to the refinery could be achieved with integrated joint-venture

[28] See the intermediate-run average cost curves in Chapter I.

[29] Bain, *Pacific Coast Petroleum Industry,* Part 3, pp. 17–18.

[30] A "balanced system" is one where an integrated company has no more pipe-line capacity than refining capacity.

lines, as opposed to singly owned lines, without appreciable sacrifices. Whether these economies could exist with common-carrier, non-integrated lines if long-term contracts were forbidden and supply were not assured is another question.

One example of an economy of vertical integration is that crude storage facilities may be minimized when the refinery has an assured steady supply of crude through its own lines. Crude inventories would be kept in the ground except for some minimum necessary for reserves in case of breakage. In the case of a joint-venture line owned by several companies which ship a different type of crude, some additional tankage might be necessary at both ends. This would be a cost offsetting to some extent the pipeline economies. However, if all companies shipped the same type of crude in a common stream, no more storage capacity would be necessary than if each had its own lines, since each could just as easily feed into and tap from the large line as from a small. Any company not able to handle an economic minimum tender in its refinery would, of course, need some extra storage (no more than it would need if the line were independently owned). However, refineries with capacities below 5000 barrels per day (Professor Wolbert's minimum) could hardly afford their own trunk lines in any case. Furthermore, if an economic minimum tender *is* 5000 barrels, then each participating refinery larger than this might well use segregated shipments and still need little extra tankage. For example, each of six 50,000-barrel-per-day refineries could feed a different 50,000-barrel tender into a 300,000-barrel-per-day line daily and tap its refinery capacity at the other end daily. Since its daily throughput capacity would be tapped in four hours (1/6 of a day), it would need additional tankage only for the other 5/6 of a day. Such a 43,000-barrel tank would cost about $45,000 [31] — an insignificant sum compared with the savings from large-line economies of scale.

It would appear that the most important advantage of individually owned, integrated lines is assured transportation, not cost savings. Assured transportation would be available under a

[31] See L. Cookenboo, Jr., "Costs of Operating."

joint-venture system. With common carriers it would be available only on a ratable-taking basis.

(8) *Access of Future Refiners.* It would appear that the establishment of joint-venture lines having exclusive transportation rights out of a field might effectively bar access to that field for any potential new refiners that might appear on the scene after the building of the line. The regulatory body would make sure that any independent desiring a share in the line (or lines) originally built would get it. But what would guarantee new independents the right to transportation in order that they might enter the field in search for crude in years subsequent to the building of the line? This might be a sufficiently serious objection to the joint-venture policy, as opposed to common carriers, to cause its rejection. If common carriers were used, then all companies, new and old, could use the transport facilities on a ratable-taking basis. Each shipper would be entitled to have a pro rata share of his offerings carried in the line (provided there were rigid enforcement of the common-carrier status of the lines). In reality, however, this problem is not of any great importance.

In the first place, if the original pipe line could carry the capacity production of the field, there would be sufficient pipe-line capacity in existence for all companies producing or purchasing in the field. If the field were being produced at capacity, then a new independent (or major) could only buy crude formerly taken by some other company (by offering superior terms). In this event the pipe-line capacity formerly used by the old purchaser would be available to the new purchaser. Would it be given to him? Since a penalty system is to be provided for failure to use one's share of the line (see the discussion of nuisance interference on page 148 above), there would be a direct economic incentive to the company having excess pipe-line capacity to let the new purchaser use it at approved common-carrier rates. Should this economic penalty not be deemed a sufficient incentive, then the permit might stipulate that any owner of the joint venture who had any excess pipe-line capacity must offer this to all takers at approved common-carrier rates. Note that this would *not* require an owner to let others use his line when he could use it (as the Wolbert plan would); this would only be done when he had unused capacity. This requirement would, of course, only apply to capacity operated by integrated companies as private carrier facilities. If the new purchaser bought oil which had formerly been carried on a common-carrier basis (if such facilities were available in the line), then the transportation facilities would be available on the same basis. Whether the purchaser were new or old would be irrelevant.

If the field were not being produced at capacity, but the original pipe line were large enough to carry the field capacity, then any new purchaser would still have sufficient transportation capacity available. It is in the case where the original line does not have sufficient capacity to carry the field capacity subsequently developed that a new purchaser might be able to buy oil and find no transportation capacity available. This case will only exist when the new field capacity has been developed by companies which did not participate in the joint venture. (If the participants developed the new capacity, they would be expected to create their own new pipe-line capacity by adding new stations if they intended to use or sell the oil at the same time that the original deposits were being utilized.) Such a situation is not likely, since late-comers might well find the desirable acreage in the field already leased. However, it is at least possible that new producers or refiners might make substantial discoveries in a field in which they were not early participants. In this event, they might build their own new pipe line. However, there would have to be a substantial amount of crude and a number of companies involved in order to get lines large enough to permit transportation at costs approaching those in the original line. Alternatively, the new entrant might be admitted to the joint venture. This could be done by expanding the capacity of the pipe line through the addition of more stations. If the line were large originally, the addition of a considerable amount of new capacity could occur without increasing per-barrel transportation costs. Indeed, substantial additions could be made with *decreased* per-barrel costs resulting to all participants, since the design capacity of any line will be to the left of the minimum point on its intermediate-run average total cost curve. If the capacity increases were quite large, the average costs per barrel might rise somewhat; this increase would have to be borne by the new entrants into the joint venture.

Should the regulatory agency have the power and duty to force the joint venture to admit new members? A prerequisite of compulsive admission of new members would clearly be the payment of certain costs and penalties. Although there is no economic reason for making a late-comer pay anything more than the marginal (incremental) cost of carrying his oil (in this case the cost of the new stations), an extra initial payment would be necessary to avoid chicanery. Otherwise, a foresighted refiner might find it worth his while to evidence no interest in a line until others had built it at, say, an initial cost of $70 million. If he needed 10 per cent of the line's throughput, it would have cost him something over $7 million if he had joined the line initially. If he waited and were not forced to pay a share of the initial cost, he could get his throughput by paying for, say, four more stations at some $600,000 each — a saving of about $4½ million. A payment of part of the initial cost is, therefore, a necessity if an injustice to the original owners is to be prevented. Initially, the new-comer should make a payment to the other companies equal to its percentage share of throughput multiplied by that part of the initial cost of the line which is not amortized when the new firm enters. In addition, something more should be charged to compensate the original builders for taking the original risk. Otherwise, an independent refiner might well wait two or three years after the building of the line to see if a new bonanza were in reality a bonanza. If not, he loses nothing; if so, he pays his share and has avoided a risk taken by the original participants. After the new-comer begins to participate he would contribute his share of the average operating cost per barrel of the line if the per-barrel cost were less than formerly. He would also pay the entire additional cost per barrel if the new throughput resulted in increased per-barrel operating costs.

The effect of this is that the new-comers would pay either marginal or average cost, whichever is higher, plus something for the risk they avoided by not participating originally. (Some time limit would probably have to be put on the risk penalty, since a refinery organized, say, ten years after the building of the line could hardly be accused of waiting to avoid the danger that the field might not be a prolific one.) However, it is necessary to ask, as did an oil company executive who read the manuscript of this monograph, whether new-comers should be forced on the joint venture under any conditions. Why should the original participants who took the high initial risk be forced to admit others a few years later, particularly in the case of companies existing when the line was built, when the field has been proved and the extra risk has disappeared? To this end, this writer would be willing to make the risk penalty for companies entering in the first, say, five years the difference between the cost of building their own facilities and participating in the joint venture. This would avoid uneconomic building of new lines, and it would also protect the original risk takers. In any event, apart from those desiring to dodge risks, the problem would only exist where there is a greater field capacity than pipe-line capacity and where the new capacity was developed by companies entering the field after construction of the line. This is an unlikely situation and, as such, is not sufficiently important to justify the use of some other policy than the joint-venture system.

(9) *Legality under the Antitrust Laws*. The final question to be discussed is the problem of legality of joint ventures under the antitrust laws. As was indicated above, it would be indefensible to force a company to refrain from building its own pipe line and to participate in a joint venture if participation in the joint venture would make it subject to prosecution under the antitrust laws, or even if it were subjected to adverse public criticism for monopolizing. While it should be apparent that the purpose of the joint venture is to minimize costs and remove any power that might exist to monopolize through ownership of transportation facilities, pipe-line joint ventures have (see page 137) been sub-

jected to criticism on this ground. Furthermore, the possible charges of monopolization have caused some companies to refrain from participating in pipe-line joint ventures in at least one important case. The adverse publicity would not be so much of a problem if such a policy were adopted with the elimination of monopoly as its aim, but there might still be a conflict with the antitrust laws.

The only important relevant decision is that in *United States* v. *Terminal Railroad Association* (1912).[32] This case involved a suit by the government to break up a joint venture of fourteen railroads controlling the St. Louis Union Station, the approaches to the Mississippi River bridges into St. Louis, all trackage on other geographically feasible approaches to the city, and most switching and delivery trackage and locomotives within the city. Such a joint venture was admitted by the Supreme Court to be economically desirable, indeed necessary, if the St. Louis gateway were to function efficiently, since wasteful duplication of facilities was avoided. However, the court found the joint venture to be a violation of the Sherman Act since it constituted an unreasonable restraint of trade.

The unreasonableness arose primarily from the fact that there were twenty-four railroads which used the terminal, but only fourteen which owned it; the ten nonparticipants in the joint venture did not receive equal treatment, either among themselves or to that accorded the owners. The test of reasonableness set up was as follows:

> Whether such a venture is a facility in aid of inter-state commerce or an unreasonable restraint forbidden by the act of Congress, as construed and applied in U.S. vs. Standard Oil and U.S. vs. American Tobacco[33] will depend upon the intent to be inferred from the extent of the control thereby secured over instrumentalities which such commerce is under compulsion to use, the method by which such control has been brought about, and the manner in which that control has been exerted.[34]

[32] 224 U.S. 383.
[33] 224 U.S. 383, at 395 cites 221 U.S. 1 and 221 U.S. 106 respectively.
[34] 224 U.S. 383, 394–395.

In this case, all participants and nonparticipants were forced to use the facilities because of geographical limitation on access to St. Louis. The participants obligated themselves both to use the system and to exclude potential competitors from acquiring interests (unanimous consent was required for new members).

> That the instrumentalities so combined are not jointly owned or managed by all of the companies compelled to use them is a significant fact which must be taken into account for the purpose of determining whether there has been a violation of the anti-trust act.[35]

The court concluded that discriminatory terms upon nonparticipants who were forced to use the terminal facilities by both economic and geographical considerations constituted unreasonable restraints of trade. However,

> It cannot be controverted that, in ordinary circumstances, a number of independent companies might combine for the purpose of acquiring terminals for their common, but exclusive use. In such cases other companies might be admitted upon terms or excluded altogether. If such terms were too onerous, there would ordinarily remain the right and power to construct their own terminals, but the situation in St. Louis is (geographically) most extraordinary, and we base our conclusion in this case, in a large measure, upon that fact.[36]

Do the pipe-line joint ventures fall into the reasonable or unreasonable category? Does it matter under current interpretation of the Sherman Act? Would possible violation of the Sherman Act retard companies from participating in joint ventures in the future?

The pipe line would effectively exclude, as has just been noted, in section 8, those who were originally nonparticipants only if the field capacity became greater than the pipe-line capacity and if these companies were unwilling to pay for their share by paying the cost of new stations plus some compensation to the other companies for their assumption of the initial risk. They are not, though, completely and finally excluded and the case is unimportant. Subsequent potential competitors would, however, be

[35] 224 U.S. 383, 404.
[36] 224 U.S. 383, 405.

under economic compulsion to use the line, since rail freight competition would be impossible in all probability because of its higher costs. The St. Louis case is not quite the same as this one, however, since there is no conscious, premeditated barring of future competitors. Furthermore, a new line could be built if the field size were to increase appreciably. The terminal could and did handle other roads without straining its capacity; the pipe line has a given capacity that can only be increased by further capital outlays. If companies which appear subsequently are willing to make these outlays, they are not excluded. The intent, if it matters, is clearly not exclusionary.

Another point is that all companies which use common-carrier, outside-financed parts of the line (if any) would not necessarily get the services at the same costs that the participating oil companies do. They would be paying rates sufficient to yield a return fixed by the regulatory agency, while the participants would pay the operating costs and an interest or opportunity cost (which might possibly amount to more than the public utility return, although this is unlikely since the opportunity cost on the companies' own pipe lines is low). It should be reasserted that any company which refuses to contribute to the initial cost cannot expect subsequent equal rate treatment; when it uses carriage facilities built with other people's money, it should pay for that use.

All this may now be of only historic importance because of the effect of recent decisions on the rule of reason. This is not the place for consideration of the current trend of antitrust decisions.[37] Suffice it to say that there is considerable doubt whether the rule of reason still applies to single firms after the *Aluminum* and second *Tobacco* decisions, although it may have been revitalized by the *Times Picayune* decision.[38] If it does not apply to

[37] See, for example, E. S. Mason, "Current Status of the Monopoly Problem in the U.S.," 62 *Harvard Law Review,* 62 ff. (1949); M. A. Adelman, "Effective Competition and the Antitrust Laws," 61 *Harvard Law Review,* 1289 ff. (1948); Rostow, "Entry," and *National Policy.*

[38] See *Times Picayune et al* v. *U.S.,* 345 U.S. 594 (1953).

single firms, then Justice Lurton's extension of it from single firms to joint ventures would probably no longer be acceptable to the court. Therefore, it is possible that joint ventures might well be illegal per se. Until such a case is brought to trial and decision, no definite pronouncement can be made (if then).

In any event, joint-venture pipe lines have been constructed in the past and are being constructed today with the approval of at least part of the Federal government — regardless of their legality under the Sherman Act. However, even recent construction of joint-venture lines may no longer be an accurate indicator of industry feelings. The Trans-Arabian Pipe Line, a joint venture by several large integrated companies, was supposedly encouraged by a part of the government. It is now an integral part of the Mutual Security Administration's suit against these companies.[39]

If joint ventures, and therefore mass transportation, are either illegal or discouraged under current interpretation of the antitrust laws, then the antitrust laws are *ipso facto* encouraging small, uneconomic lines. If this be true, some exemption from the Sherman Act should be granted. Where rates are regulated, as in the case of public utilities, and exclusion of competitors is not possible, such exemption should be objectionable only to those who favor smallness for its own sake, regardless of the economic cost.

Summary. Any public policy for crude oil trunk pipe lines should insure:

(1) That conglomerate mass transportation will be used to the greatest possible extent in order to achieve minimum costs for all companies.

(2) That all market-oriented, non-integrated refiners, existing (to the extent that there are any) and potential, should have access to crude without dependence on the transportation facilities of integrated companies, in order that entry into refining may be on its own merits.

[39] See *World Oil*, September 1952, p. 52. The MSA objects to the rate of 66 cents per barrel (based on a 5-year pay-out of the investment).

This can best be accomplished by a compulsory joint-venture system embracing all companies, large or small, which are willing to pay a share of the initial outlay. Non-integrated refiners who are unwilling to accept a share can use any common carrier facilities owning interests in the line. These might not materialize, but they are no less likely than if completely non-integrated capital had to be obtained to build large-diameter common carrier lines. Indeed, outside interests would probably be more likely to participate since smaller sums could be invested in several lines (thereby spreading the risk) and since the assistance of major-company credit ratings would be available.

Enforcement of the system might well be unnecessary in most cases for two primary reasons: (1) there is an existing, unregulated movement in the industry toward large joint ventures (indeed, the latest such joint venture, Trans-Mountain, is an almost ideal example of how a pipe line should be built); and (2) there is a real economic incentive, lower costs, for combined transportation. If the majors themselves really believe their repeated assertions that they own pipe lines for good economic reasons and not to control other stages of the industry, then they would have no reason to exclude any bona fide applicant from a joint venture.

In the rare cases where there might be a dispute over refinery terminals for competing joint ventures from a new large field, a regulatory body might have to make a choice in the interests of preventing wasteful use of steel and excessive costs. Otherwise the regulatory body would not deny the right to build line. If made, such a decision would be subject to court review — in other cases a decided disadvantage because of the time involved; but this review would be most desirable in such circumstances. The necessity of delaying court review in cases other than this type would probably be negligible.

Companies desiring to participate after construction of the line could do so by paying for additional stations (if needed) and part of the initial costs, plus a penalty for avoiding risks.

If there is a conflict between such joint ventures and the antitrust laws, specific exemption should be provided, since this would be a clear case where the antitrust laws were discouraging (1) low-cost facilities, and (2) entry of small firms into the industry. Furthermore, it would be indefensible to require firms to participate in joint ventures if they are illegal.

BIBLIOGRAPHY OF BOOKS AND ARTICLES CITED

BOOKS

Bain, J. S., *Economics of the Pacific Coast Petroleum Industry* (Berkeley, Calif., 1944–1947).

Boulding, K. A., *Economic Analysis* (New York, 1941), 1st ed.

Chenerey, H. B., Engineering Bases of Economic Analysis (Cambridge, Mass., 1950), unpublished thesis deposited in Widener Library.

Cook, R. C., TNEC *Monograph* No. 39, *Control of the Petroleum Industry by Major Oil Companies* (Washington, 1941).

Haberler, G., *Prosperity and Depression* (Lake Success, New York, 1946).

Hicks, J. R., *Value and Capital,* 2nd ed. (Oxford, 1948).

Hughes, G. C., The Preliminary Design of Crude Oil Trunk Systems (Austin, Texas, 1949), unpublished thesis deposited in the Library of the University of Texas.

Fair, M. L., and E. W. Williams, Jr., *Economics of Transportation* (New York, 1950).

McLean, J. G., and R. W. Haigh, *The Growth of the Integrated Oil Companies* (Boston, 1954).

Robinson, E. A. G., *Structure of Competitive Industry* (London, 1935).

Rostow, E. V., *A National Policy for the Oil Industry* (New Haven, Conn., 1948).

Sybert, J. H., The Economic Selection of a Crude Oil Pipe Line (Austin, Texas, 1948), unpublished thesis deposited in the Library of the University of Texas.

Wolbert, G. S., Jr., *American Pipe Lines* (Norman, Okla., 1952).

United States Department of the Interior, Petroleum Administration for Defense, *Transportation of Oil* (Washington, 1951).

United States Temporary National Economic Committee, *Hearings,* Part 15 (Washington, 1940).

ARTICLES AND PAMPHLETS

Adelman, M. A., "Effective Competitive and the Antitrust Laws," 61 *Harvard Law Review* 1289 (1948).

———, "Integration and Antitrust Policy," 63 *Harvard Law Review* 27 (1949).

Cookenboo, L., Jr., "Costs of Operating Crude Oil Pipe Lines," *Rice Institute Pamphlet,* April 1954.

Coombs, A. T., and I. F. Avery, *Crude Oil and Refined Products Pipe Mileage in the United States,* United States Bureau of Mines Information Circular (Washington, 1950).

Hill, E. G., "Engineering Economics of Long Petroleum Pipe Lines," American Institute of Mining and Metallurgical Engineers, *Transactions,* Petroleum Division, *Petroleum Development and Technology,* 1942, pp. 231 ff.

Kennedy, W. L., Jr., and C. G. Stueve, "Sizing Crude Oil Pipe Lines," *Oil and Gas Journal,* September 21, 1953, pp. 183 ff.

Mason, E. S., "Current Status of the Monopoly Problem in the United States," 62 *Harvard Law Review* 62 (1949).

Oil and Gas Journal, March 17, 1952, pp. 321–339.

Petroleum Refiner, "Box Score" of refinery construction, appearing quarterly.

Rostow, E. V., and A. S. Sachs, "Entry into the Oil Refining Business: Vertical Integration Re-Examined," 61 *Yale Law Journal* 856 (1952).

Sheve, W. H., "Electric Power for Pipe Lines," *World Oil,* June 1949, p. 87.

Stigler, G. S., "Extent and Bases of Monopoly," Supplement Number 2, Part II, *American Economic Review,* 1942, p. 1.

United States Interstate Commerce Commission, *Statistics of Oil Pipe Line Companies* (Washington, annual publication).

Young, F. R., "Applied Design and Economics of Pipe Lines," *Oil and Gas Journal,* November 8, 1934, pp. 38 ff.

INDEX

Bei Fragen zur Produktsicherheit wenden Sie sich bitte an:
If you have any questions regarding product safety,
please contact:

Walter de Gruyter GmbH
Genthiner Straße 13
10785 Berlin
productsafety@degruyterbrill.com